Beyond the Veil: Our Journey Home *by 1*
about dying. It's the personal, right-here-and-
set it apart. This wealth of "what really works" comes from her own experiences
when she died and returned a near-death survivor, and from her years since of
serving at the deathbed in a ministry of love and forgiveness. There are so many
books out now about how to help the dying, but nothing like this. Her "Personal
Transition Guidebook" that she helps the dying to create becomes a precious gift
— a way for individuals to consciously prepare for what's to come, and to better
understand the life in their death, and what happens next. Anyone can benefit
from this book, so, keep it handy. You may use it more often than you think.

> P.M.H. Atwater, L.H.D., researcher and author of *Near-Death Experiences: The*
> *Rest of The Story, The Big Book of Near-Death Experiences,* and *We Live Forever:*
> *The Real Truth About Death*

Diane Goble's book, **Beyond the Veil: Our Journey Home,** *shows us how*
learning to die consciously not only soothes the transition for the dying but
also makes for a better grieving experience for those left behind. There is no
easy way to bring up the conversation of death but Goble's book shows us why
this discussion is one of the most important discussions that we can have.
Unfortunately, when we arrive at the end of our time in this lifespan, the
physician is likely to write us a prescription for hospice and send us off to die.
The physician will generally see our death as a failure instead of realizing that
death is a necessary part of an ongoing cycle of life. It is a process that still
needs their full attention. We can help both doctors and our family and friends
by making sure they know what our wishes are.

> Josie Varga, Author of *Visits from Heaven & Visits to Heaven*

Diane Goble's book, **Beyond the Veil: Our Journey Home,** *is a must read*
for everyone really, as at one time or another in your life, you will be faced with
conversations and decisions about death and dying. Being prepared will help
take the edge off the anxiety and tensions that are experienced amongst family
members and close friends. Giving these topics serious thought before or during
the process is a powerful way to feel more empowered and in control of the
situation. I love the way Diane uses meditations and guided journeys to assist
us in engaging more deeply with the Art of Conscious Dying. They helps us to
flow more easily through the transition stages from our dense physical forms
to a more profound connection with our Soul Essence. Ultimately learning
how to be fully present and conscious for the one who is passing is one of the
greatest gifts you can offer someone you Love. Diane offers some of the most
comprehensive, well thought out and practical information available on this
subject. A truly valuable read.

> JoAnn Chambers, Vibrational Sound Healer and co-author of *The Sonic Keys:*
> *Sound, Light & Frequency, DNA Activation and The Secret of Abundance*

Beyond the Veil

Beyond the Veil

Our Journey Home

2nd Edition

Diane Goble

∞

CosmicCreativity
Sisters, Oregon USA

1st Edition (ebook): How to Die Consciously: Secrets from Beyond the Veil (2011)

Large Print

Front Cover Artwork by PJHunterDesign.com
Book Cover Design by JoAnnChambers.com
Typography by JoAnnChambers.com

ISBN 978-0-9638-606-5-1

PUBLISHER'S NOTE

෨ை

ACKNOWLEDGEMENTS

I'm eternally grateful to my spirit guides and master teachers for helping me put this information into a coherent whole, and to my friends Kelsey Collins, Linda Depee, Linda Lenton, Melissa Maher, Maggie Saslow, Sue Stafford and my Certified Transition Guides Terri Daniel, Dar Umemoto, Chrystal Wadsworth for their feedback, editing tips and loving support.

DEDICATION

This work is dedicated to all those who yearn to remember who we really are, why we are here and what comes next so when they graduate from this University of Life on Earth, they do so with a higher consciousness than they came in with.

৵৽৻

Eventually it became clear to me that more people have had such experiences—truly secret voyages into a reality separated from this one by a flimsy veil of disbelief—than not. Parting the veil means changing your own perception. This is a personal, totally subjective, yet very real shift.
~ Deepak Chopra, "The Book of Secrets"

CONTENTS

Do not stand by my grave and weep.
I am not there, I do not sleep.
I am a thousand winds that blow.
I am the diamond glints on snow.
I am the sun on ripened grain.
I am the gentle autumn rain.
When you awaken in the morning's hush,
I am the swift, uplifting rush
Of quiet birds in circling flight.
I am the soft star-shine at night.
Do not stand by my grave and cry.
I am not there, I did not die.
~ Mary Elizabeth Frye

Preface

We all know we're going to die — some day. We just don't want to talk about it or think about it but it's always there — that fear lurking in the background, that monster waiting to strike. The Grim Reaper coming to take our loved one or us away. It's in the news headlines everyday. We can't escape it.

As a child, I remember having an intense fear of death and no idea of what "death" really meant. I knew several of my 90-something year old great grandparents briefly and then they just didn't come around anymore. My mother's grandmother died in her sleep in the bedroom next to mine unbeknownst to me. Her father dropped dead of a heart attack a few months after he retired. A car speeding through the crosswalk in front of my elementary school hit a classmate. She just never came back to class. Nobody said anything later. It seemed to me people just disappeared and were never seen again. I wondered where did they go?

I began to fear that my parents would suddenly disappear, and my younger sister, Bobbie, and I would be orphaned. When they went out for the evening, I would sit at my window watching for their car, unable to sleep until they were safely home. We had a big oil-burning furnace in the basement. I feared it would explode and burn the house down with all of us inside. I had a great fear of fire.

I don't know where the fear came from unless it was just that I was born during WWII and my father was in the Navy... and there was talk about the Holocaust, Pearl Harbor and the atomic bomb... and duck and cover drills at school when the air raid sirens went off scaring the crap out of everybody that the Russian bombers were coming. I doubted my desk was going to protect me.

Then a month before my 11th birthday, Bobbie died. Accidentally killed when she was standing too close behind another 8-year old when he swung his golf club hitting her in the head. She apparently stumbled down the fairway to the 18th green where she collapsed and never regained consciousness. I wasn't with her when it happened. I didn't really know what happened but was whisked away from the country club on Long Island, NY, by a family friend to a waiting room in a hospital... where Bobbie and I played as usual, practicing for our next ballet recital, until someone came in and told me she had died.

Huh?

It was my first funeral. I remember my father lifted me up next to the white satin-lined mahogany coffin where she lay to kiss her goodbye and her skin was cold as ice. I didn't understand. Nobody warned me about that. Totally freaked me out. I had nightmares about being buried alive for years.

Nobody talked about death. In fact, in my family it seemed nobody ever talked about Bobbie again. It was as if she never existed. We moved to another house in another city and didn't bring anything with us from the past. My parents had two more children. We moved on, but I knew they never got over her death. I lived in a state of confusion.

In middle school, I began to study various religions and attend various churches looking for answers about the mysteries of life and death. As a teenager, I found some solace in Catholicism. I graduated from high school, went away to college for a couple of years, got married in the Church, and had three children baptized in the Church. Then I left the Church after a disagreement over the birth control issue.

After my third child, my doctor said not to get pregnant because I had fibroid tumors and needed a hysterectomy. My priest said I had to make up my own mind about birth control so I did and figured if I could make these kinds of decisions myself I didn't need to go to church anymore. I became more of an agnostic, a secular humanist, not believing in anything, not going to any church. I didn't give death a second thought — until I drowned on July 18, 1971, two months shy of my 30th birthday.

My husband John was a member of a motion picture crew filming the movie *Deliverance* on the Chattooga River in northern Georgia. A group of eight of us took two rafts out to have our own white water adventure on a hot Sunday afternoon, which was great fun until we made one little mistake that trapped our raft in a hydraulic at the bottom of a waterfall surrounded by large boulders.

I'm going to share some of my near-death experience with you because it explains how I got into this work and is the source of my knowledge about the Art of Conscious Dying. Much of what I'm going to share about the journey home may conflict with your beliefs, but don't throw the baby out with the bathwater — you're likely to find this information fits nicely into most belief systems since it comes from the same source as all of them. It gives people some practical things to do when faced with a pending death in the family.

I suddenly found myself stuck between a rock and a hard place, trapped by what local river men called a "keeper hole," and I knew there was no way out. I was going to die. But instead of feeling terrified, I was very calm, very peaceful. Time slowed way down. I was thinking quite rationally and logically about which would be the better way to die and chose drowning over being pummeled to death into the rocks.

Someone still inside the raft was holding onto my arm while my body was outside the raft repeatedly being sucked down and pushed up by the raging water. I caught a quick breath and yelled, *Let go!*

He did.

There was no struggle to reach the surface, no panic to breathe or not breathe. I just inhaled the water, calmly surrendered to the river, and everything went black — just as I had every reason to believe it would. I had no belief in an after life.

But then something quite remarkable happened. It was as if I had simply closed my eyes and then opened them again, but instead of being under the water, drowning, I was floating high above the forest and the river, looking down at the raft and all the people who were gathering around the scene at the river's edge.

I saw John looking around frantically for me, jumping out onto a rock, ready to jump into the river to try to save me, but I knew it was no use because my body was trapped under the raft and I was, well... not in it.

With that thought, I instantly found myself by John's side, reaching out to stop him, but my hand passed right through his body and he showed no reaction. That was when I realized I must be dead and there was nothing more anyone could do here.

I felt myself being suddenly pulled away from the river and forest, and the earth environment quickly disappeared. I seemed to be traveling through an endless darkness, moving through something like a tunnel or vortex towards a beautiful, brilliant golden light a zillion miles away.

I could see streams of lights rushing past me as I moved forward at the speed of light. Or was the light moving closer to me? I wasn't sure whether I was moving or the lights were moving, or both, or neither.

There was no wind or sense of movement. No sound. It seemed to be a timeless state with no apparent motion, yet I seemed to be getting closer to it, expanding, becoming one with this light. There was nothing uncomfortable or frightening about this. Instead, I felt I was surrounded, wrapped in blissful feelings of unconditional love beyond anything I experienced on earth.

I sensed the presence of a Being of Light traveling beside me. I don't know who it was, perhaps my guardian angel. Immediately I realized I had always known this being, and that this being knew everything about me and still loved me unconditionally. There was no moral superiority or judgment. It had no discernable shape, no gender. I was filled with peace and joy... amazing grace.

We communicated telepathically, without sound or words. Each question that came to me was answered immediately, before I could even ask it. It was more like I was remembering things I already knew rather than receiving new information.

I laughed to myself for not remembering while I was in my body that this is how it all works. This is our journey home. It all made perfect sense in that instant, and I thought how different life would be if, while embodied, we remembered that there is no death. It is all just a continuum of life in different forms, in different realities, always changing, always evolving.

Everything suddenly made complete sense. I remembered that we are not human beings who have a soul; we are souls who incarnate as human beings so we can experience life and relationships in the physical world. I saw the Source/God as an eternal, living, changing, evolving system of being and becoming. "God" is everything we can't see when in body but when our body dies, the veil drops and we see clearly the reality that lies beyond our human senses.

Humans do not have souls that lie in wait on some other side to then be judged and punished or rewarded for eternity, as some religions would have us believe. Nor are we insignificant, useless beings who live short, purposeless lives on planet earth only to die and turn to dust, as atheists insist.

We are eternal Beings of Light who come and go from the spiritual world to physical worlds, from our spiritual essence in and out of physical bodies, as the experiential part of our soul's eternal journey evolves.

Subsequent to each physical lifetime, our soul consciousness returns to Source to integrate new learning and knowledge into the collective consciousness, which contributes to the evolution of human consciousness and the raising of our individual vibration to a higher frequency of light.

I know, what the heck does that mean? It made perfect sense to me at the time!

I remembered everything I had forgotten, including that I had done this before — made this transition many times — and that I was a Being of Light/Soul having just returned from another human experience. Reincarnation, which I had previously viewed as an amusing concept, suddenly made perfect sense to me.

It's not about who we were in another life, how much money or things we accumulated, or how powerful we became; it's about involvement of spirit in the evolution of human consciousness.

Souls incarnate as sentient beings, not to become more powerful humans, but to become more powerful expressions of Unconditional Love in the physical world. Not to become domineering and controlling or accumulate wealth and property or become powerful bankers, or political or religious leaders, but to practice kindness and compassion toward our fellow humans and all life on the planet.

We are learning to balance our humanity with our divinity, to evolve our consciousness by recycling and purifying our energy as we learn to express Unconditional Love in the world. Or as Jesus said more succinctly, *the meek shall inherit the earth!*

The Bible suddenly made complete sense. I had read it before as stories and metaphors, and not understood its deeper meaning, but now I saw clearly that it was just interpreted differently by different religions, as are all descriptions of the afterlife, based on the level of consciousness of the observer. But regardless of who is observing or interpreting, it all comes down to one truth: God is the Love in the Light and we are All That!

As I got closer, the Light grew brighter and more intense, yet I could look directly into it without recoiling. "God" is Unconditional Love and, as a prism separates white light into a spectrum of colors, every thing is projected from this Clear Light. God is Pure Consciousness, without human qualities or desires, constantly creating the Ground of Being.

God is not a big guy with a long white beard sitting

on a throne surrounded by a choir of angels being worshiped by hoards of disembodied souls waiting to be judged. There is no God that demands sacrifice or chooses one side over another in human battles for wealth or territory, nor promises rewards to those who kill others in God's name. Religious zealots, oligarchs and kings make all of that up to control populations by fear and intimidation.

Suddenly I could see beyond the veil. A million colors sparkled like jewels in a field of diamonds as I moved into the Light and merged with it. An environment was revealed before me, more beautiful, more colorful, more vibrant and more alive than the most beautiful scenery on earth. Not a landscape but a celestialscape. There was light everywhere, but no sun, no clouds, no sky. No darkness. No shadows. Only variations of light far beyond the color spectrum we are able to see with human eyes. Without eyes, we are able to see so much more.

With the Being of Light as my tour guide, we traveled (flew, floated) to many different areas where I saw incredible scenes and living beings of light going about their daily lives. If something caught my attention and I wanted to know more about it, I only had to notice it and I was immediately transported — or it appeared closer to me. With the thought *what's that over there?* Whoosh! It was in my face (so to speak, as I didn't have a face).

I was shown healing centers and halls of learning where I observed newly arriving souls being acclimated to these surroundings before they were ready to return to their families. They were being attended to by spiritual healers who were using light and energy to ease their fears and help them remember who they really are and how the universe works to clear up any misunderstandings they acquired during their human lives due to erroneous information. Many of these souls had been so deeply entrenched in the physical world and their emotions, they were unable to recognize their true selves during their journey home and would need more time to acclimate.

In another area, souls preparing to reincarnate into new physical bodies were being helped by their soul family to make decisions about the circumstances of their next lives, relationships and families. Decisions that would help them work through the lessons they failed to learn in previous lives (karma) as well as new lessons about being both Human and Divine while in a physical body. I remembered this is the perfecting or purifying process every soul goes through as part of its eternal spiritual journey just as I had done so many times before.

After exploring and refreshing my memory about the activities of souls in this dimension, the Being of Light reminded me how to increase my vibration and guided me to another light frequency where higher learning takes place. I was told I had been "recalled" home because I had a special "mission" in this life, but it seems I had drifted off-course.

We telepathically discussed my return to my body, which now seemed to me to be *Diane's* body and I had no interest in it, as we were approaching what I perceived to be a cluster of crystal structures, which appeared to grow larger and more complex. From afar, they shimmered like a mirage on hot desert sand. As we drifted closer, it appeared to be a crystal city. We settled at the foot of the most prominent conical-shaped tower, which was now so tall I couldn't see its pinnacle.

I was told this was the Hall of Knowledge and that if I chose to return to Diane's body, I would be given information to bring back with me. My mission was to be a messenger and share this information with others, to help human beings grasp the important but misunderstood concept that *we don't die.* Our physical body dies, but who we were before we were born and while our bodies functioned, survives bodily death.

I was told this information would not only accelerate individual souls along their spiritual path, but accelerate the evolution of consciousness of humanity, which is the path to peace on earth.

Though reluctant to leave this beautiful, loving experience, I was all in favor of contributing to world peace. With simply that thought, I suddenly found myself being pulled toward and into this amazing crystal tower, and spiraling upwards through what appeared to me to be shelves of books and scrolls, apparently absorbing knowledge as I went.

I suddenly burst through the top of the tower into a slow-motion shower of multi-colored, sparkling crystal shards and, *at the same instant,* my head burst out of the water in the river! The roar of rushing water all around me suddenly shattered the peacefulness I had enjoyed during my journey beyond the veil.

I was back in my body 100 yards downstream from the raft, which was still stuck in the keeper hole with one man still inside. I quickly grabbed on to the nearest rock to gather my wits and noticed the other man and woman from our raft were hanging on to rocks nearby.

I had no memory of my body tumbling about under the raft or coming out from under it, or trying to breathe or struggling to hold my breath under water. I also had no memories of being swept along by the current through the treacherous rapids, around boulders and fallen trees, to the calm pool below where I ended up, basically without a scratch.

As soon as my head popped out of the water, I was aware of being back in my body and in the river. I was totally conscious and had no need for resuscitation or medical attention (a good thing since we were deep in the forest, miles from civilization).

I was speechless and astonished, and had no words to articulate what I had just experienced. John, who had successfully transversed the same rapids ahead of us in another 4-person raft, later told me I mumbled something about having been somewhere, but nothing else coherent.

Remember, this was 1971 — before Dr. Raymond Moody wrote his book *Life After Life* in which he coined the term "near-death experience" (NDE). I didn't realize other people had had these kinds of experiences until 15 years later when I came across another book describing other people's out of body and into the Light experiences. Until then I was afraid to talk about it because when I did, people looked at me as if I'd lost my mind. I didn't know what had happened to me. I didn't even know what to call it.

The river men said I survived because I surrendered to the river. As I remember how cold the water was and from my subsequent studies into the NDE, I think my physical body may have gone into hypothermia and just shut down until I was safe to reanimate. Imagine that!

However, the instantaneous switch from one reality to another and back again — suddenly observing the scene from above, and then crashing through the top of a building and my head popping out of the water at the same instant, and how I recovered consciousness so quickly at that instant, is all quite a conundrum. I didn't know it then and not for a long time after, but this experience was my *deliverance.*

My experience of life continuing beyond the veil certainly relieved me of my fear of death. It also showed me how to help others overcome fear of death by helping them remember that *there is no death* except of the temporary physical body we wear while on earth. We go on. Life goes on. Love goes on. The adventures continue!

It has become my soul mission in this life to assist during humanity's transformation to a higher state of consciousness *as I've come to understand it* over the four decades since I left my body.

To me this has come to mean that as humans we need to get beyond our egocentric, ethnocentric, earthcentric behavior and thinking. Thanks to Science, we now know that Earth is not the center of the Universe — our solar system is not the center of a galaxy — the Milky Way Galaxy is not the center of the Universe — and the Universe is multidimensional.

The vastness of "All That Is" is pretty much beyond the human brain's current ability to comprehend, but humans are not stuck at this level. The evolution of consciousness involves us remembering as humans that we are more than human — we are also fundamentally powerful spiritual beings capable of endless possibilities for creation in an evolving physical universe.

All I ask is that you open your mind and suspend your judgments as you read this book the first time, then run it through your critical thinking filter. Discard what doesn't fit and build a stronger, more sustainable foundation on what does.

Step One is remembering that we are all spiritual beings having human experiences and at the end of each human lifetime, our journey home is the continuation of our ongoing, eternal spiritual lives.

We don't die when our body dies, we simply go through a transition from one state of awareness to another. We simply step out of our body, bid our loved ones goodbye for now and move into the arms of our loved ones waiting beyond the veil. We have returned to our home in the light from which we came. This knowledge allows us to prepare ourselves for our transition whenever or however it happens.

It is not meant that this book be read only once but read again and again over the years. Each time you read it, you will find deeper meaning and greater comfort in times of need. Hopefully it will help you to live this life in peace and joy with freedom from any trepidation about dying or death.

The information herein was gleaned from my experience beyond the veil to share with those who are ready to put it into action in their lives. If I occasionally sound authoritative, it is not my intention; it is my writing style. (I'm not trying to start a new religion or to discredit any existing ones.) This information comes strictly from my personal experience and studies trying to make sense of it for myself, as well as to help others *remember* and find peace of mind such as I have.

This book has been condensed from a more extensive training course that I developed in 2007 to introduce professional and paraprofessional healers, hospice caregivers, nursing educators and ministers to another way of looking at death and dying.

As Certified Transition Guides they are trained to teach this process, and help their clients reconcile their lives well before their deaths and compose their own "Personal Transition Guidebook" (Chapter 6) to comfort them during their transition process.

This print version, I consider a 2nd edition to my ebook *How to Die Consciously: Secrets from Beyond the Veil* (2011). As long as I had to get the text ready to be published in paperback, I wanted to add more up-to-date information about the Death With Dignity laws and changes concerning end of life care over the past few years. I did do some editing and added a chapter about how to do guided visualizations, otherwise there is not a lot new in this version. Although it had been my best selling ebook, I've changed the title in hopes of being able to share this information with a wider audience.

This handbook is applicable to everyone whether they are sick or perfectly healthy because for all of us, physical life, at some point, will end, but it is particularly germane to those who have received a diagnosis that has even the potential to be terminal or who are becoming frail from advancing age. It is also for their caregivers who can be helpful family transition guides by preparing their dying friend or loved one for their last great adventure in this life.

This method of conscious dying is non-religious, nondenominational, but based on spiritual concepts, and may be adapted or used in part with most any religious practice or without religious rituals. Every religion has its own name for the conscious field of energy that created or caused everything in the observable universe to exist and its own dogma defining who or what that is. They all contain some truth.

These myths and stories are all attempts to explain the same single source, which are then labeled for common understanding (God, Allah, Jehovah, etc.). I neither condone nor dismiss any of them, nor suggest that I have the definitive answers. Throughout this book, I will interchangeably use some of these names all referring to the Source of our existence. Please feel free to substitute whatever name brings you comfort.

In practice, this method may only involve the dying person or include the whole family and support team as active participants. It is flexible enough that even an atheist may find some comfort from having given it some attention once he finds himself out of his body and still conscious, especially in the case of sudden death.

If you are the soon-to-be departing person due to age or illness, you could read this handbook, develop your own plan, practice it on your own, and compose and record your own Personal Transition Guidebook. However, you may find it more comforting to enlist a friend or caregiver to work through the steps with you, help you compose and practice reading your Guidebook with you, and be there to read it to you during your transition, which is its purpose.

It's easier to practice the guided imagery exercises when you have another person to read the scripts to you. Especially with your Personal Transition Guidebook, hearing another person's voice during your transition will keep you from being distracted by the wonder of your experience and whatever images, pleasant or unpleasant, may arise in your consciousness.

I mention *unpleasant* experiences because it seems the thoughts one dwells on most often during their lives, as well as one's thoughts at the time of transition, are carried over in consciousness and negative thoughts may manifest in frightening mental images, described by some NDErs who encountered them as "hellish." Keep in mind that these are "mental" images and cannot hurt you. You are no longer in a physical body.

I would also suggest that the person you choose as your transition guide be impartial or at least not be someone so emotionally attached to you that he or she is unable to let go or be supportive of your last wishes.

Sometimes in this book I'm talking to or about the person acting as the transition guide and sometimes I'm talking to or about the person who will be departing. Hopefully readers will not be confused about which one I'm referring to at the time.

The *Introduction* describes the near-death experience and the information I received about transitioning during my NDE. Current literature concerning the survival of consciousness after death is also discussed.

Chapter 1 provides information to help family members have the conversations that are so difficult, yet so important to have before it is too late to have them. Documents, such as Advance Healthcare Directives, organ donation and funeral arrangements become discussions the whole family can participate in — not just for one person, but also for all members. Palliative and hospice care options, and the current Death With Dignity laws are also discussed.

Chapter 2 discusses end of life in terms of "transition," not dying, which makes the last part of life an ongoing adventure, not the end of it. I discuss the value of working with a transition guide as a personal assistant to prepare oneself for a peaceful process of reconciling one's life through forgiveness and gratitude work, purifying one's energy field, and practicing letting go of earthly attachments. There are ideas for the transition guide, the family and the person leaving about how to make it the most loving, compassionate experience for all concerned.

Chapter 3 contains the elements of the practice of the art of conscious dying. There are sample scripts for the transition guide to read to the person leaving that teach a simple meditation/relaxation exercise that can be helpful to anyone, but especially for people preparing for transition to help them get comfortable with this practice while they are still capable of doing so. There is also a purification script, which helps clear accumulated toxins and traumas so the soul may exit the body through the top of the head directly into the Light.

Chapter 4 looks at working with the subconscious mind and gives some guidelines about writing your own scripts for guided meditations, which may relate to one's life review, creating an inner workspace to do the necessary work to prepare oneself for a peaceful and joyful transition, and imagining one's journey home beyond the veil. As a Certified Clinical Hypnotherapist, I offer tried and trusted guidelines for working with the subconscious mind.

Chapter 5 discusses the practice of the art of conscious dying, and how it can be helpful for people emotionally and psychologically as they undergo treatments, procedures, and surgeries to keep their bodies alive. You'll learn how guided visualizations can be used to facilitate reconciliation and help a person get in touch with her spiritual self.

Chapter 6 explores the origins of Books of the Dead or funerary texts from ancient to modern day cultures as background. It is a guide to help people compose their own transition guidebooks using their own words to assist and comfort them on their journey home.

Each chapter is followed by a page or two for notes as this book is intended to be used as a notebook.

A sample of a *Personal Transition Guidebook* is included to provide readers with suggestions they may want to include in their own Personal Transition Guidebook to keep them from being distracted by what may actually occur during their transition. It is merely a template upon which you can lay your own personal beliefs about the transition process and what comes next. Above all, it should be in your own words, according to your own beliefs.

In the *Appendix*, readers will find a list of questions that can be used to encourage a person to review his life and deal with karmic issues before taking leave so they won't need to be encountered during one's life review on the other side — which is what the guided imagery exercises and Personal Transition Guidebook are designed to do.

Also in the *Appendix* for those interested in *Death With Dignity Laws*, current U.S. laws are provided. There is a great deal of debate going on, in Europe as well, so check on progress where you live with CompassionandChoices. org. You'll also find samples from the Egyptian and Tibetan Books of the Dead to show how far we've come from the mysterious to the practical. And finally there is one of my favorite poems, *The Blind Men and the Elephant,* which makes the point that we tend to stay stuck in our own perspective and need to step back to see the bigger picture.

You can't see the picture when you're in the frame!

NOTES · NOTES · NOTES · NOTES · NOTES

NOTES · NOTES · NOTES · NOTES · NOTES

Introduction

"We are not human beings having a spiritual experience.
We are spiritual beings having a human experience."
~ Pierre Teilhard de Chardin

Lessons of the Near-Death Experience

The near-death experience has become a popular subject on radio and TV talk shows, as well as scientific research, since Dr. Raymond Moody wrote *Life After Life* in 1975. He reported then that only about 10% of people who are resuscitated report any conscious memories during the time they were apparently dead but since then millions of people have reported some kind of experience beyond the body and continue to do so.

There is a difference between nearly dying or coming close to death and having a near-death experience. I've personally had several occasions when I nearly died or came close to death, but I've only had one NDE. Even the out-of-body-experience (OOBE) is only part of what is considered a "core" NDE, which, according to Moody and other researchers (Drs. Ken Ring, Bruce Greyson, Melvin Morse), includes some or all of the following descriptions:

- An overwhelming feeling of peace and well being, including freedom from pain
- The impression of being located outside one's physical body
- An experience of universal or total knowledge
- Floating, drifting or speeding through darkness, sometimes described as a tunnel.
- Awareness of a welcoming bright golden light
- Encountering and perhaps communicating with a "presence" or "being of light"
- A rapid succession of visual images of one's past; a life review
- Experiencing another world of much beauty, brilliant colors, beautiful music
- Meeting religious figures or deceased relatives and acquaintances
- Reaching a point of no return, being given a choice to stay or return.

With these descriptions being so common among millions of NDErs, there is good reason to consider they are giving us insight into at least the beginning of what we get to experience consciously as we leave our body and the physical world behind, and return to our spiritual home and family in the Light.

In my case, I believe my NDE was not so much about me (I didn't experience a life review), but about my spiritual mission. I was taken further beyond the veil than most NDErs report.

The teachings I absorbed as I spiraled through the Hall of Knowledge, which I later integrated during my formal education 7 years after my NDE and for another 7 years after I earned my master's degree in Community Psychology studying the great philosophers, yogis and Ancient Mystery Schools, were necessary to help me reveal ideas about the Divine in more relatable and unbiased terms.

None of this insight made me into a saint or prophet or guru or expert in anything profound. I'm not a member of any religious group. I don't go to any churches. I'm not trying to start a new religion but I am hoping to add to our conceptual framework about who we are and why we're here. It did broaden my understanding and give me the ability to see the bigger picture; however, I don't claim to have all the details.

My wisdom is still filtered through my human brain, which is still fallible. The information in this book comes from the depths of my experience and 37 years of study and meditation into the Nature of Reality, both scientifically and in higher states of consciousness.

It doesn't seem to be important on the other side which religion we followed during our life, or whether or not we believed in God or Allah or Buddha, or were an atheist. We are all welcomed home. But whatever our inner beliefs are, that is what we will experience, at least during the early part of our transition. Some

NDErs report this as comforting, others as frightening, depending on their thought patterns and state of mind at the time.

It does seem to be that we carry our baggage (unresolved karma, emotional attachments, lessons not learned or unfinished business) with us when we go, which results in a life review. We get to experience the mistakes we made and the kindness we showed to others to help us with our life lessons.

The implication is that we need to forgive and ask forgiveness, resolve anger and bitterness, and express gratitude where necessary during our lives. Even our last thoughts before we die follow us and influence our journey. Being filled with fear or anger or love is a choice we can make.

Karma is not a system of rewards and punishments. It is not about fate or pre-determination. It is about learning to be loving and compassionate in all circumstances and relationships. It is about the life lessons our soul decided to explore before it came into this life and whether, as humans, we master them or not.

We are presented with opportunities and challenges in this life to help us learn. We could be learning about patience or tolerance, success or failure, wealth or poverty, addictions or health issues. We choose our gender, our relationships and families, our environments and nationalities, our religions, our circumstances, to experience what our soul needs to evolve in consciousness.

While the lessons our soul wants us to learn are planned before birth, the choices we make in the situations we attract in the physical world are the human's to make (free will). We are only accountable to our soul for the *intentions* behind our actions during our life review.

The outcome is less important (e.g., if one is here to study wealth, achieving wealth is not a measure of success — the means by which she achieved her fortune and what she did with it are.) Whether she was selfish or charitable, giving or a hoarder, determines her karma.

Lessons learned result in raising the frequency of our light vibration and the level of our consciousness during transition. When we don't learn a lesson, it holds us back, presents us with even more difficult challenges to get us to wake up, and keeps us coming back to try again in different circumstances as different human beings in different relationships, usually within our soul group. We reincarnate together to help each other evolve.

To be clear about reincarnation, it's not "Diane" who keeps coming back. She is a one-time incarnation of a soul who returns home with new insights about the physical world that are integrated into the whole of her being. Her soul's next incarnation might be as a man in China or a woman in Peru who may or may not have some of *Diane's* personality traits and may or may not be dealing with some of *Diane's* unresolved karma.

This is all decided in pre-birth planning and is related to what the soul hopes to learn through its next human lifetime. *Diane* is part of something greater than her self, but not by any means insignificant to the whole.

Most NDErs report being given a choice about returning to their body and many of them, including myself, were reluctant to do so. It's important for those living in-body to realize that when the choice to not return to that body is made, it is the soul making a decision to evolve beyond this human experience, not the human personality making a choice to leave his family behind.

This choice involves the soul's pre-life plan as to how long to remain in a particular human body to learn what it incarnated to learn through this life experience. We may well have a number of possible exit points, occasions where we could decide to leave or stay to do more work or dissolve more karma through further human experiences. Sometimes a life review or a future vision is revealed to help with the decision to return or not.

In the case of suicide, the pre-birth plan may have included this option for the person to grapple with and we may all have wrestled with it in more than one lifetime, depending on the decisions of our human beings. People who have survived a suicide attempt and had an NDE often report they now understand why suicide doesn't solve anything and is a waste of a life opportunity — a setback in soul growth. They may experience a life review that shows the person the affects of their suicide on their family or a future scenario showing what they might have learned from this lifetime if they had not attempted to end it.

We who are left behind grieve the loss of our loved one because we don't understand or accept that her death is necessary to her soul growth. It's difficult to cheer someone on when we can't see the graduation ceremony, which from her perspective is what happened when she left her body.

I called my NDE a *mid-course correction* necessary to get me onto my spiritual path. My inclination was not to return to Diane's body, but my soul had other plans. It was definitely the turning point for Diane in this lifetime.

When the choice is not to return, lessons have been learned, mission has been accomplished, life has been reconciled and issues resolved to some extent. It's time to evolve to a higher level of consciousness through another incarnation. Perhaps one learned all one needed to in that life, no matter how short.

Our soul knows those loved ones left behind in the physical world will be with us again in the blink of an eye on the other side of the veil where there is no time or separation. We are all on this miraculous journey together, though we are not always physically together.

The death of our human body is another opportunity for our soul to graduate from the "University of Life on Earth" with a greater awareness about existence as a conscious-biological being in a physical environment.

When our human body dies, we shift or transform our energy or vibration to a higher frequency of light and continue along our eternal spiritual journey. On a conscious level, it is as if we closed one door when we became human and opened another when our human died. When we recognize this, we can begin to write our Personal Transition Guidebook accordingly.

Just as we are adults containing the child and teenager we once were within, we are a soul containing all the personalities from our past lives. As spiritual entities, we are able to recognize each other as we appeared in previous lifetimes as human personalities depending on the circumstances.

At the same time we are One with the Divine, we are also individual souls manifesting in many dimensions in many different forms. To visualize this heady concept, consider the *Matryoshka*, or Russian Nesting Dolls, that have similar, progressively smaller dolls within the other. Or consider the onion — peel off one layer and there is a similar, smaller onion within, down to the core.

NDE Research

Many dying people have reported descriptions similar to NDE stories as they came close to death; some right up to their last breath. Dr. Elisabeth Kubler-Ross, a pioneer in the field of death and dying, recorded some of these stories as she sat with hundreds of patients, including children, in hospitals as they were dying.

She wrote about her findings in a number of books, including *On Death and Dying: What the Dying Have to Teach Doctors, Nurses, Clergy and Their Own Families,* and concluded:

> *Death is simply a shedding of the physical body, like the butterfly coming out of a cocoon. It is a transition into a higher state of consciousness, where you continue to perceive, to understand, to laugh, to be able to grow, and the only thing you lose is something you don't need anymore —your physical body. It's like putting away your winter coat when spring comes.*

Kubler-Ross' research shows that people who are

dying appear to be able to see and communicate with entities that can't be seen by people in the same room who are not dying. Medical people insist the dying are hallucinating from the morphine or their brain shutting down because the science-minded are unable to perceive the veil, much less see beyond it. How is it then that NDErs and dying patients often see loved ones they didn't know had just died or recognize someone who died before they were born?

Hospice nurses Patricia Callanan and Maggie Kelley confirmed Kubler-Ross' reports in their book, *Final Gifts: Understanding the Special Awareness, Needs and Communications of the Dying*. They shared similar experiences with dying patients over their years as hospice nurses and concluded:

> *One of the most important aspects of Nearing Death Awareness is the need for reconciliation. Dying people develop an awareness that they need to be at peace. As death nears, people often realize some things feel unfinished or incomplete — perhaps issues that once seemed insignificant or that happened long ago. Now the dying person realizes their importance and wants to settle them. If this awareness comes late — when death seems imminent — the person may delay or prolong dying in an attempt to affect a reconciliatory meeting.*

Journalist Josie Varga in her book *Visits to Heaven* presents dozens of NDE accounts and chapters written by experts in the field of NDE research to help people arrive at their own conclusions. My account starts on page 12 in her book. She writes:

*All NDErs say that they don't believe there is life
after death; they know it. Likewise, they don't believe
there is a God or Supreme Source; they know there
is. They also know that we are much more than our
physical bodies. We are eternal beings connected in
Oneness with a purpose.*

Dr. Bruce Greyson (*The Handbook of Near-Death
Experiences: Thirty Years of Investigation*) at the
University of Virginia and Dr. Kenneth Ring (*Lessons
From the Light*) at the University of Connecticut
conducted scientific studies into NDEs and NDErs to
develop an objective model.

Dr. Melvin Morse (*Closer to the Light: Learning from
the Near-Death Experiences of Children*), a pediatrician,
interviewed hundreds of children about the experiences
they had when they suffered cardiac arrest in the hospital.
These scientists all conclude that these experiences are
real and there is more to life than meets the eye.

Researcher, author and three-time NDEr, PMH
Atwater, has studied the subject extensively and written
numerous books, including *We Live Forever: The Truth
About Death*. After interviewing over 4,000 NDErs she
reports:

*It's not quite what we've been told. You have to go
further. There is no life after life or life before life;
there is only life... always life no matter what form
you are in.*

Current scientific research into NDEs is concentrating
on making a case for the survival of consciousness after
death. Dr. Pim van Lommel, a Dutch neuro-psychiatrist,
who studies near-death experiences of cardiac patients,

in his book *Consciousness Beyond Life* states:

> *The conclusion that consciousness can be experi-*
> *enced independently of brain function might well*
> *induce a huge change in the scientific paradigm*
> *in western medicine, and could have practical*
> *implications in actual medical and ethical*
> *problems such as the care for comatose or dying*
> *patients, euthanasia, abortion, and the removal of*
> *organs for transplantation from somebody in the*
> *dying process with a beating heart in a warm body*
> *but a diagnosis of brain death.*

Dr. Peter Fenwick (a British neuro-psychiatrist) and Elizabeth Fenwick, in their book *The Art of Dying*, describe accounts by the dying and those who were with them in their final hours to help us understand the process of dying. From their research, they suggest those who have gone before us are there to help us during our transition from this life to the next. Since there is no rational explanation for this, it appears the current scientific view that consciousness is brain-based cannot be sustained and that something — soul, spirit or consciousness — continues, at least for a while. They say:

> *You should be ready to die at a moment's notice.*
> *Those with a clear conscience die well. Those who*
> *are angry or frustrated have a much more difficult*
> *death.*

Dr. Sam Parnia, a colleague of Dr. Fenwick's and a critical care doctor in a British hospital emergency room, became interested in some of his patients' accounts of experiences they reported while clinically dead and began conducting his own experiments into what NDErs see or hear going on around them when they have clearly flat lined and there is no brain activity on the monitor.

Picking up where Dr. Raymond Moody left off, Dr. Parnia wrote *What Happens When We Die: A Groundbreaking Study into the Nature of Life and Death,* in which he laid the groundwork for his further studies into the survival of consciousness. He placed placards with pictures on them near the ceiling at specific places in a number of hospitals hoping people who have NDEs will be able to describe them. His study is currently under peer review and should be released this year.

This idea was based on one patient who described seeing a tennis shoe on a building ledge during her NDE, which was later found as she described it. He explains:

If there were, say, five images and someone identified all five of them, it would be almost impossible statistically for it to happen by chance alone.

In the United States, Dr. Jeffrey Long (a radiation oncologist) began a web site (NDERF.org) several years ago and asked NDErs to fill out an extensive questionnaire about their NDEs. It has now become the largest NDE study ever conducted with thousands of participants. His interpretation of the database can be found in his recent book *Evidence of the Afterlife: The Science of Near-Death Experiences.* My experience is included on pages 76-8 in his book.

Dr. Long breaks down his evidence into nine categories, such as the remarkable consistency of the details of NDEs around the world, the accuracy of the life reviews that occur during NDEs, and the transformational effects these experiences have had on the lives of those who have them. Dr. Long concludes that we now possess the most compelling evidence for life beyond death ever compiled and that:

NDEs have been a message of hope to millions of people that there is an afterlife for both themselves and their loved ones. With the latest scientific NDE research... this message of hope about the afterlife is becoming a promise.

NOTES · NOTES · NOTES · NOTES · NOTES

Chapter 1

> "I'm not afraid of death; I just don't want to be there when it happens."
> ~ Woody Allen

End of Life Conversations

There is no easy way to bring up this conversation with your spouse or your parents, or even a friend. Many physicians find it uncomfortable talking to patients about end of life treatment and care issues. Only in recent years have some medical schools included a hospice rotation in their programs to expose students to pain management and the dying process.

Today, when physicians run out of treatment options or the patient decides no more, the physician is likely to write a prescription for hospice and he'll never see that physician again. Generally, physicians see "death" as a failure, not as part of an ongoing process that could still benefit from their expertise. At the end of treatment, we need midwifery skills to rebirth the soul.

We all need to have some of these conversations with our health care team and our family <u>before</u> we need to have them so that by the time we do need to have them, it is easier to make decisions. Mentioning this book or giving it to someone you know who is getting older or has been dealing with an illness that has the potential to be fatal is a way to help get the conversation started. Introduce it with how it helped you or a friend.

If you are helping someone prepare their Advance Directive, ask, as part of the conversation, if they have thought about end of life care and how they would prefer to spend their last days, and if they would be interested in reading a book to give them some ideas to think about.

This is not a one time and forget about it conversation either. Just as our views about life and death change as we age, our thoughts about what we would want at the end of our lives tend to change as well. We may think differently at 70 than we did before we were 60 and could still do most of the things we loved to do. One might want to review his last wishes and final arrangements paperwork every five years, and more often as he grows older or his health changes.

Just as we need to plan ahead for end of life living arrangements by visiting appropriate assisted living facilities to help in the decision-making process when new health care and caregiving for physical and/or mental conditions become an urgent concern for a family member, we need to consider what we will accept as far as medical treatments and emergency interventions as our health condition changes.

Writing an Advance Directive brings up a lot of thoughts and can be a good time to open discussions about what people want to consider in the way of treatments and care, living conditions, caregiving, family support and where they want to die.

Once everyone has the information and the forms in hand, it is easier to have a reasonable discussion about the many possible contingencies and talk about what one will accept or not accept as far as treatment near end of life (e.g., resuscitation, feeding tube, hydration, life support). It's even less threatening if done as a family group discussion where opinions can be aired and everyone is clear about what each other wants.

There may be some strong differences of opinion about end of life healthcare decisions and some heated arguments may ensue. In the end, it has to be about honoring the departing person's wishes. This is another reason to have these discussions before they are necessary and without the added stress of a sudden medical crisis. Decisions can be further discussed and refined over time rather than at the same moment life or death decisions are being made in the Emergency Room or ICU. Some people put off thinking about any of this until it happens.

Countless studies have shown that extensive medical interventions can make the last weeks of life an excruciating experience for patients and those who care about them. It's not just the elderly who need to have this conversation. Certainly everyone over 18 needs to consider their wants in case a life or death situation occurs. Parents need to have a discussion about their young children if one of them should become seriously ill or injured.

Some people will choose to prepare themselves while they are young and healthy so that whenever they die, however it happens, wherever they are, they will know what is going on as they are leaving their body, what options they may have once out of body, and what to do next. This is "conscious dying."

Not *conscious* meaning awake, that would be nice but doesn't always happen, but deliberate and intentional, under one's control, aware of what's going on and pariticpating in the process.

Waiting until you are near death to accept that you are going to die, may keep your transition experience from being as awesome as it could be. Not knowing what to do or even that one has just died, may cause great confusion and missed opportunities to evolve in consciousness upon leaving one's body.

Whether you believe life continues after the death of the body or not, if it does the information will be beneficial to you. If you're right that there is no afterlife, it won't matter but you will have lived a more loving and peaceful life in the meantime.

After you get a diagnosis that you have a life threatening illness, there may be little time to learn to practice dying consciously. It's not that it takes a lot of time, maybe 30 minutes a day while you're learning, it's that everything else that goes with treating an illness is so overwhelming and before you know it, there is no more time. It's one of those things better learned before you need it so it will be there for you when you do.

While we had gradually acknowledged to each other that he might not make it, we'd never really accepted it or talked about what it meant. I always thought we'd have a period of time when he was in hospice care when we would talk more and say our goodbyes. While I, and my kids, said lots of goodbyes and I love yous while he was in a coma, he was never able to communicate with us again. I still replay those last few days over and over and wonder how we didn't know he was so close to the end and wonder if he knew.

~ Kathy's story

A study in the *Archives of Internal Medicine* (2009), disclosed that the costs of care during the last week of life were 55% higher among those who did not have end of life discussions with their doctors. Also the quality of life in their final days was much worse than among those who did have such discussions.

Even more important than how your estate is to be settled is what are your end of life healthcare choices. Studies show that 40% of people have not yet thought about advance healthcare planning and 90% haven't documented their wishes for end of life care (*The Journal of the American Geriatric Society, 2009*).

You've been in an accident. You're transported by ambulance to an emergency room. You're unconscious. Life or death decisions have to be made immediately. Your heart stops, do you want to be resuscitated? Under what circumstances? What if there is an 80% chance of full recovery? What if it's only 10%? What if you're

90 years old or dying from cancer? You're in a coma for weeks, months, years. You're in a persistent vegetative state with little hope of recovery. Would you want to be kept alive on machines and feeing tubes for a week, for a month, indefinitely? How will your loved ones know what to do if you don't tell them beforehand or write down your last wishes?

The Terry Schiavo case showed every person who heard about it the value of deciding what we would want long before it becomes an issue. If you suddenly become incompetent, unable to make decisions for yourself, due to circumstances beyond your control, someone is going to have to be your voice. You better hope they are advocating for your wishes, instead of their own agenda, beliefs or culture.

Mrs. Schiavo collapsed at age 27 from sudden cardiac arrest and suffered severe brain damage from lack of oxygen in 1990. After a few months her condition was elevated to vegetative state and she was kept alive by a feeding tube. Her husband petitioned the court to remove the feeding tube in 1998 but her parents insisted she was conscious and recognized them. It turned into a 7-year legal battle that made national headlines. The tube was removed then reinserted by court order.

The second time it was ordered removed, U.S. President George Bush got involved and signed legislation to reinsert. It was finally removed in 2005 and Mrs. Schaivo was allowed to die peacefully. An autopsy later revealed she had irreversible brain damage and was blind. (Wikipedia.com)

It is difficult to pinpoint when we start dying because

we actually start dying at the cellular level from the moment we are born. We usually assume it starts at the time we are given a prognosis of six months or less to live because we have a disease process that can't be stopped by medical science.

Sometimes, even with that shocking news, some people believe they will survive. They may stay adamantly in denial until the very end. They say there is always hope so they don't prepare themselves for their death. People don't want to talk about dying because they don't want to be seen as giving up. For some, suffering is rather like a badge of honor or a religious imperative.

People don't want to accept hospice because they think it means giving up when, in fact, it gives them quality time with their families for the last few months or weeks they have left and a more peaceful, gentle transition experience than they would have in busy, noisey, brightly lit hospital intensive care unit.

In fact, many people do so well under hospice care that they get better and are able to outlive their diagnosis with a better quality of life than they had while undergoing drastic measures trying to keep them alive with the same outcome. They will still die, but while doing what brings them joy... not greater anxiety and suffering.

The alternative means:
- Invasive medical procedures
- Drug interactions and side effects
- Reoccurring hospitalizations
- Calls to 911
- Resuscitations
- Stronger drugs, more side-effects

- More drastic procedures
- Less quality of life
- Briefer periods of remission less often

Only 17% of patients brought to the ER for resuscitation from a heart attack survive to discharge (*CPR Survival in Hospital Setting,* eperc.mcw.edu/fastFact/ff_179. htm). 80% of patients die in the hospital on life support, many after someone has had to make the decision to pull the plug, instead of peacefully in a comfortable bed at home surrounded by the love of family, friends and compassionate caregivers.

Some people are afraid if they talk about death, it will happen. No, talking about it does not make it happen, but *not* talking about it makes it a worse nightmare for everyone involved. Accepting that death is one of several possible outcomes opens the door to begin to prepare yourself, mentally, emotionally and spiritually, while you are still somewhat healthy and coherent, for whatever happens, whenever it happens.

More often than not, death comes as a total surprise and no one, including the deceased, is prepared for all that comes next. Everyone is in shock, unable to comprehend what has happened. These days, while texting, one could fall into a sink hole or step into the street and get hit by a bus.

Depending on our circumstances, we each have more or less time to live. We may have a slow, progressively worsening condition from which we deteriorate over years or a sudden trauma that results in immediate death or death a short time after an accident. We may have a sudden heart attack or aneurysm and our life is over in a matter of seconds. We may go in for a routine surgical procedure and never wake up. We may slip into a coma and languish for years in a vegetative state.

There are many ways it could happen. The only thing for sure is that, one day, it will!

People, who start this practice of conscious dying long before they get sick or die suddenly, are always prepared when it does happen. It will be instinctual when you need it most — an immediate reaction without having to wonder where am I, what the heck just happened, and what do I do now?

Practicing with your loved ones deepens the bond of love between you, as you become companions in this shared sacred journey. It takes only your time in the beginning; in the end, it could be down to a few words, a sound, a simple chant. For the rest of your life, it will remain like a beacon in the darkness, there when you need it.

Your specific end of life wishes should be recorded and kept with your final papers so there is no question about what you would want depending on the circumstances. Give copies to your health care representative, doctor, nursing home, anyone who needs to know what you want and don't want. It's also a gift to your loved ones left behind rather than leaving it up to them to make decisions when they are also in a state of shock over whatever has happened to you.

Studies show that grief is mitigated when people discuss end of life choices with their dying loved ones beforehand. These people weren't left to agonize over whether they did what the person would have wanted at the end of their lives (AARP, 2010). Having to decide whether to take a person off life support without knowing what they would want is a terrible burden to force on a loved one. They will appreciate knowing what you wanted and not having to wonder or feel guilty after the fact about whether they did the right thing.

Talking about Death

There is a new tend toward encouraging people to have these conversations about death and dying, end of life care and filling out Advanced Healthcare Directives long before there is an immediate need. Physicians are asking their patients to have these conversations early in case of an emergency situation. Emergency medical personnel encourage patients to discuss *what ifs,* just in case.

Small gatherings are happening around the country for this purpose to help people become more comfortable talking about this topic because it has been kept in the dark far too long. It used to be that people died at home surrounded by family. Now death often happens in ICUs or nursing homes where people find themselves confused with medical terms and procedures they don't understand, and are forced to make life and death decisions without ever having talked about it among family members.

Death Cafes started in Europe and have taken hold in many places in the U.S. The idea is to get together with a small group of people over dinner or tea and cake, and talk about death. There is no agenda or list of topics. Anything to do with death is appropriate.

The hope is to get people more comfortable talking

about death so they can begin to have the important conversation with their family members. While there are many local groups appearing more frequently, there is a web site, deathcafe.com, where you can search for one near you or start a group yourself.

TheConversationProject.org has a starter kit with questions to encourage participants to think about what kinds of life-saving treatments they want and don't want, and what they want their death to be like. There is more detailed information about filling out one's Advanced Healthcare Directive and discussions about end of life care options. Ask yourself, how do I want the end of my life to be?

Death classes are also being offered at community colleges and local hospices sponsor community programs about their services including palliative care and filling out Advanced Healthcare Directives. With all the changes in healthcare and insurance, and medical advances, you owe it to yourself and your family to educate yourself so it isn't such a shock when it happens to you or someone you love.

Last Wishes and Final Arrangements

There are documents that should be filled out and, in some cases, notarized relating to your choices for treatments, procedures, care, medications, feeding tubes, hydration, resuscitation, end of life decisions, disposition of your body and possessions, and funeral arrangements. Ideally, these should be signed while you are healthy and of sound mind, and updated every few years depending on your health, age and circumstances.

You will need to appoint a healthcare representative you trust to take over should you become incapacitated, and discuss your desires and choices well in advance of them needing to step in, especially if you have a sudden health change (e.g., a stroke) or accident rendering you incapable of making decisions for your care.

Many people these days are also pre-planning their own going away parties, Celebrations of Life, home funerals, green burials, and anniversary celebrations. You can now even leave messages on a web site to be emailed to your loved ones after your death. Your family will be grateful for your pre-arrangements. In the meantime, you can live your life to the fullest knowing your last wishes will be carried out.

The following is a list of the documents you may need to convey your last wishes and final arrangements. Note that state laws vary and it can't hurt to consult a lawyer. Definitely hire one if there is an estate or any complicated family situation involved. Go to nolo.com or legalzoom.com to download all the legal forms you'll need and locate lawyers in your area.

Advance Health Care Directive
Some states require the use of their respective state specific forms (see Living Will and Health Care Power of Attorney); some states have unique statutory requirements regarding the form of medical directives; others have adopted specific advance directive forms —POLST (Physician's Orders for Life-Sustaining Treatment) or MOLST (Medical Orders for Life-Sustaining Treatment), which may be registered electronically and be available to hospitals.

The Advanced Healthcare Directive document combines the best features of the Living Will and Health Care Power of Attorney. When signed by a competent adult (a "Declarant") in advance of serious illness or accident, it provides directions regarding health care that should (or should not) be provided to the Declarant if the Declarant is unable to communicate his wishes.

Declarant may state:

- Whether life-sustaining procedures should be withdrawn or withheld so that you can transition naturally if you have a "terminal condition" or are in a "permanent coma"
- Whether "artificial nutrition/hydration" should be provided to you if you have a "terminal condition" or are in a "permanent coma"
- What procedures (e.g., chemotherapy, kidney dialysis, cardiopulmonary resuscitation, use of respirator) you do or do not wish to receive
- Whether you have made arrangements to donate organs or your body to science
- What consideration shall be given to you and your fetus if you are pregnant
- Other provisions that limit or expand the document (e.g., regarding access to medical records, authority to perform an autopsy)

The Declarant retains the right to make his own health care decisions as long as able to do so. The document only becomes effective when you do not have the capacity to give, withdraw or withhold informed consent regarding your health care. Once capacity is restored, authority returns to Declarant.

Living Will

A document under which a competent adult, prior to becoming unconscious or incompetent, declares his intention that life-sustaining procedures should be withheld or withdrawn under specified circumstances. The Living Will should not be confused with the Simple Will or the Living Trust. The Living Will is related to the Health Care (Durable) Power of Attorney document.

Health Care (Durable) Power of Attorney

A document which allows an individual ("Principal") to designate another individual ("Agent") to make health care decisions for the Principal if the Principal is unconscious, incompetent or otherwise unable to make such decisions. The document may also contain information to guide the Agent in making health care decisions for the Principal. "Durable" means the document is only effective during any period of time that the Declarant is not competent.

If you become competent again, you are back in control.

Compassion & Choices

Compassion & Choices is a nonprofit organization that offers consultation, planning resources, education, referrals and guidance to help everyone have the best death possible.

On their web site at compassionandchoices.org you will find state-specific downloadable forms for end of life planning, including Advanced Healthcare Directive, Dementia Provision, Assisted Living Facility Rider, Sectarian Healthcare Directive, Values Worksheet, A Letter to My Doctor, and an Unwanted Medical Treatment Toolkit.

Organ Donation/Anatomical Gifts

Making a gift of your body can be done by several methods: a bequest of particular organs for transplantation, donation of all organs and tissues, or the donation of the entire body or brain to a medical school. Alternative disposition preferences should also be made if the donation cannot be completed for any reason. There may be a charge if you want the cremains returned to you.

Wallet-size donor cards are available from local agencies, such as hospitals, the local office of the National Kidney Foundation, or a community eye bank. Some states provide organ donation check-off on driver's licenses. Also inform family members or close friends to assure fulfillment of your desires.

To donate the whole body, the school or hospital to which such donation will be made should be contacted ahead of time. The institution will advise of their particular procedures and can provide you with the necessary forms.

The dissection of human bodies is an invaluable part of medical school training and scientific research. A donor form may indicate whether the Declarant prefers his body be used for anatomy classes or for scientific research. Bodies generally are rejected if they are decomposed, obese, emaciated, amputated, infectious, mutilated, have been recently operated on, autopsied, or are otherwise unfit. With the exception of corneas, organ donations cannot be made if the body is to be donated to medical science.

The cost of donating a body to medical science may include a minimal fee for transportation of the body. Some schools will pick up the body. Donation of a body to science is the most economical disposition of a body. A special embalming process is required. The body is kept from six months to two years. Upon completion of the medical studies, the remains are generally cremated. Some schools will return the body or cremains, sometimes charging for any costs incurred.

Donations can be made of a variety of organs: liver, heart, kidneys, bones and tissue (including cartilage, marrow, skin, eardrums and corneas). Human tissues include pituitary glands, brain tissues, middle ears, ear bones, heart valves and other organ subparts.

Two physicians with no interest in the transplant must find the patient "utterly and irretrievably deceased." After being declared brain dead, the organ donor is placed on a respirator until the organs are removed.

Refusal to Donate Organs

If you decide you do not want to donate any organs, be sure to fill out a Refusal to Donate form revoking any previous organ donation forms and have it properly signed and witnessed. Inform your family and physicians. Carry it in your wallet.

Funeral Home Arrangements

You may want to make selections and desires known to a funeral director or at least visit one and get their information. You might also consider home funerals and green burials. The information gathered now will make it easier for family members to make decisions when they are necessary.

Some funeral homes and memorial parks offer prepaid funeral plans. If you make prearrangements, choose a reliable funeral director (one whose business you would expect will still be in existence at the time of your death). Also, be sure that your funds are paid into a state-regulated trust fund. This assures that the funds are available when they are needed. Verify how this fund is handled and what happens to your prepayment if the funeral director's business is sold or the director goes out of business.

If such a plan is chosen, you should be sure to attach proof of such purchase to this document. A description of pre-need arrangements will be necessary to assure that your loved ones know which items you have already paid for.

As you make your plans, find out if adjustments can be made at the time of your death. Some pre-need plans permit you to transfer the arrangements from one funeral home/cemetery to another. You should also ascertain if a pre-purchased lot might be transferred or sold if circumstances change.

When choosing a casket, consider that there are a variety of prices within each type of the various materials from which they are crafted; it is not just the material that determines the price. Funeral providers are prohibited from misrepresenting protective features of caskets, outer burial containers, vaults and grave liners, which is another reason to pre-plan rather than your family having to make a hurried, uninformed decision. Providers may also not imply that the law requires a casket for direct cremation, which it does not, and are required to offer inexpensive alternate containers.

Many funeral homes will provide pallbearers at an extra charge; certainly family members and friends may be pallbearers. In places like New York City, the pallbearers union requires paid professional pallbearers, unless you can obtain a waiver.

You may also decide which clothes you want to be buried in, what kind of grave marker or urn and what you want written on it, what your obituary will say, who will be invited to your funeral, and anything else you want to make decisions about beforehand.

Funeral homes or the County Health Department will provide certified copies of the death certificate signed by an attending physician or coroner. The executor will need to send proof of death to collect survivor or death benefits, claim life insurance proceeds, manage the decedent's assets, probate or execute the will, and prepare fiduciary tax returns. They may need to be sent to banks or brokerage firms, pension or retirement accounts, Social Security, Veterans Affairs and other agencies or organizations.

Determine the number of copies you will you need before ordering, as the cost of the first copy is more than each additional copy, depending on the state —each time you place an order, so I suggest ordering at least one or two more than you think you'll need, just in case.

If you have questions about the laws in your state, you may contact the licensing board that regulates the funeral industry in your state. If you have a problem concerning funeral matters, first attempt to resolve it with your funeral director. If you are dissatisfied, contact your local consumer protection agency.

Home Funerals & Green Burials
There is more we can do to take back control of our lives

and our deaths. The Funeral Industry has taken over care for the dead, but that began as a matter of convenience and we're not required to use their services. There are death midwives who will teach families how to wash the body, how to prepare the body for viewing, and officiate at a home funeral ceremony. They should also be aware of state laws and be able to handle all the paperwork, get copies of the death certificate, and arrange for disposition through green burial or cremation.

Green burials may include no embalming, cremation, or the use of a biodegradable box or shroud-type wrapping or one's favorite blanket for direct ground burial. Some cemeteries have designated natural areas where trees and flowers may also be planted to reduce the environmental impact. Some states allow burial on family acreage. One can also become part of an underwater coral reef by having your cremains mixed into a form that is then positioned underwater with others to encourage reef building.

In the future, professional Transition Guides will be able to offer a continuum of services to families, and be part of this movement to bring dying back into family life and out of the hands of government and corporations.

Treatment of the Body
This section concerns the selection of a final resting place for the body. Survivors can visit this place to mourn or reflect in a quiet, contemplative setting. Burial plots may be purchased from cemeteries, memorial parks, cooperative groups, as well as governmental agencies. Above ground burial or entombment is also an option. A mausoleum tends to serve not only as a burial place, but

may also be as a monument to the deceased individual or family.

Cremation is the reduction of the body to minerals through intense heat. The ashes and bone fragments that remain after cremation are called "cremains." These cremains are placed in an urn or other container for burial, storage or scattering. Modern day cremation artists are creating some imaginative ways to preserve your loved ones ashes.

An Internet search of "cremation artwork" will turn out a list. Examples are picture frames or boxes, diamonds and jewelry, and artificial ocean reefs. Most states allow cremains to be scattered if the bone fragments in the cremains have been pulverized. Ask a funeral director or crematorium about local rules.

Embalming involves injecting a dead body with chemicals to retard decay. State law does generally not require routine embalming; however, death from a communicable/contagious disease or transportation by a common carrier requires embalming in some states. The type of embalming used to delay funeral arrangements for several days does not preserve a body much beyond that time.

Funeral providers are required by the Federal Trade Commission Funeral Rule to provide information about embalming so that a consumer can make a more informed decision on whether to purchase this service (including that embalming is not required by state or local law for direct cremation, immediate burial, a funeral using a sealed casket, or if refrigeration is available and the funeral is without viewing or visitation).

Celebrations of Life

The purpose of this document is to leave instructions regarding your desires for your final arrangements. Memorial ceremonies are for your survivors, and they should be taken into consideration when pre-planning.

Those who make plans ahead of time relieve their families of having to make crucial decisions under the influence of grief. Gather photographs, a list of your favorite music, a journal of favorite family stories. It is best to talk about these arrangements with your family so they are aware of what you want them to do when the time comes.

Some people would prefer to have their memorial service before they transition, which could be called a Celebration of Life. Rather than have their friends and loved ones gather round and express their feelings for them after death, they would rather hear what they have to say while alive and be able to say their good-byes before they die.

Realistic planning may be difficult for an event that may not take place for many years so planning should be made on a contingency basis. Changing circumstances may require that changes be made in your plans over time. If you provide guidance to your family, and yet indicate that you understand that changes may need to be made based on their circumstances, they will likely feel more comfortable in meeting your guidelines.

If you are in the terminal stages of a disease, your needs are more immediate and you need someone you can talk to about how you want to spend your last days and how you want to die. Don't let concerned loved ones tell you you're not going to die or that everything will be all right, if you want to be in control of your own dying process. Loved ones should not dismiss the dying person's need to talk about their death.

Dying is something we all have in common, and we need to talk about it and make it a special time for expressing love and gratitude for being part of each other's human life journey.

You may have a preference for a certain spiritual or religious service, a military funeral (vets contact the VA for details, benefits, etc.) or a private family service. You may want your ashes kept in a pre-selected urn on the mantel or scattered at sea or sprinkled in your rose garden. You may want to personalize your service to reflect your life in certain ways. You may want balloons or white doves to be released, or request a Reggae band, or pass a talking stick to share stories about you around a campfire or in your favorite pub. You can have a party with lots of music and story telling.

A memorial service can be the celebration of a soul being reborn into pure joy, urged on by the laughter and tears of loved ones.

Notification

A number of alternatives are available to notify individuals and institutions of a death. Many times the immediate notification of the deceased person's clergy person permits him to assist the bereaved family and friends or you may designate a family member or friend to handle this part.

Family and close friends should be telephoned immediately. You may create a list of people and places to be notified or refer to an address book or email list. Formal printed announcements, usually used by businesses to inform colleagues or clients, maybe sent.

Public announcement of a death can be accomplished through publication in local newspapers. A death notice is a free announcement; a fee may be charged for an obituary. You may want to write your own or write down certain pertinent information to be given to a friend or relative to write it for you.

In addition to family members and friends, there will be others who need to be informed of your death; for example, banks, mortgage holders, credit card companies, Social Security, alumni association, clubs and other organizations to which you belonged. The Personal Fact Sheet identifies important information that can be used to ascertain who should be notified.

Electronic Media
This is an area no one has had to deal with until recently. Now our whole lives are online and with so much security we need to be mindful that if we were to drop dead tomorrow no one would be able to access our accounts or even know what to look for on our computer, tablet or phone. Due to privacy terms, companies cannot release your passwords.

A hardcopy list could be kept with your other end of life paperwork. All your online accounts and passwords, all your personal account numbers (banking, financial, brokerage, credit cards, loans, utility bills, etc.), your web sites, email addresses and online services, your social networking accounts and passwords, your address book, and other personal information that would be needed by your executor and family after your death. For privacy, don't list these items in your will or any document that may become public.

If you read the TOS agreement with many of the online services you subscribe to, they probably state that your account will be closed upon notification of your death.

Palliative and Hospice Care

Palliative care is a new area of specialization in healthcare that bridges the gap between hospital and hospice. It's appropriate for patients in all stages of chronic diseases, those undergoing curative treatments following an accident or surgery, and those nearing the end of life. The focus is on preventing suffering and pain management while undergoing standard medical care.

Palliative medicine utilizes a multi-disciplinary approach to patient care, relying on physicians, nurses, social workers, psychologists and integrative health care providers as a team.

The difference between standard medical care and hospice is not the difference between treating a condition and doing nothing. The difference is in priorities. The goal of ordinary medicine is to extend life (sacrifice the quality of life now for the chance of gaining time later). The goal of hospice care is to help people with end-stage illnesses or aging, who opt for no further medical treatment or procedures, to enhance quality of life now by managing symptoms and pain until they die naturally.

A person is eligible for hospice care when their doctor

determines no further treatment is available, he doesn't qualify for any more clinical trials, and he likely has six months or less to live. A person may choose to forego further medical treatments, request hospice care, and let nature take its course. The person can stay in his own home or in assisted living or be a nursing home resident or go to a hospice house depending on his physical condition and financial situation.

Many hospices now have transition teams who will help patients as they move from palliative care to hospice care and sometimes back to palliative care. Many people improve for a time under all the attention they get from hospice caregivers and are taken off hospice during this remission period. They may go back on hospice care any time their condition deteriorates.

In a study mentioned in an article in *The New Yorker* ("Letting Go" 8/2/2010), 4,493 Medicare patients with terminal cancer or congestive heart failure showed either no difference in survival time or they lived longer with hospice care. It seems "you live longer when you stop trying to live longer."

Under hospice, patients are assigned a team of nurses, social workers, chaplains, and volunteers whose goal is to make them as comfortable as possible by managing their pain until they make their transition. Volunteers offer a few hours of respite each week so the caregiver can get out of the house to run some errands or go to appointments, get a massage or a haircut, take a meditation or yoga class.

Alternative hospices offer some complementary services, such as massage, yoga, reiki, light/energy work, hypnotherapy. Hospice people are the most loving, compassionate people you'll ever meet. They will make one's last days the most peaceful of one's life. It is not giving up hope; it is accepting your spiritual path and preparing for your journey home after a life well lived with a heart filled with peace and joy!

That's the good news. Like most things, the system doesn't always work the way it's supposed to in practice. Money for healthcare is a big issue and becoming a bigger issue as the Baby Boomers age. Just when more services are going to be needed, money is flowing in the opposite direction; fewer people want to be in the medical field just when more doctors and nurses are needed. The need for home health care givers will explode to support the limited help available from the hospital system and insurance coverage.

Palliative care is being touted as being able to bridge the gap between hospital and hospice, but most hospitals don't yet offer palliative care. They don't have the budget. They don't have a staff trained in pain and symptom management. They're just not set up to meet the coming demand.

Hospices have better networks in place and many now have facilities for respite care — except in rural areas where staff is small and over-extended, and patients may live hours away. Again lack of budget, lack of staff. They are able to monitor some patients electronically and they get to their patients on their rotation but they may not be able to be there when you're loved one is dying and you need them the most.

These are issues people need to research before their

loved ones are in need of these services. These entities are different in every town and state. You're not going to be able to find all the answers you need when you're in a crisis situation and don't know what your actual choices are. Go to their offices and get information, talk to a counselor about potential needs and what services are available to you. Talk to others who have used hospice services and palliative care to find out the things to be aware of to eliminate unpleasant surprises during a health crisis.

Dealing With Our Own Death

Dr. Elisabeth Kubler-Ross gave us the five stages of grief. These refer not only to the survivor's experience after the loss of a loved one, but the experience of loss a person goes through towards the end of his life with each simple chore he can no longer do for him self. They are:

- Denial and Isolation
- Anger
- Bargaining
- Depression
- Acceptance

You might think that, at first, with a diagnosis that indicates the end is probably very near (6 months or less) that you would first go into Denial that this could be happening to you and you keep it a secret from others.

Next you go through a period of intense Anger — anger at God, anger at yourself, anger that this is happening to you. This is followed by a period of Bargaining.

You bargain with God, you bargain with the doctors, you bargain with your family. You make promises to change your behavior.

Then you fall into Depression because you can tell your body is failing and nothing that's been tried is making it better. You turn out the lights, pull down the shades, forget to charge your cell phone, pull the covers over your head and generally feel sorry for yourself.

Then, at some point, you suddenly come to an understanding with God, with yourself, with your disease, and an Acceptance of your death comes over you. You get your paperwork in order, make end of life arrangements, and get about the work of dying.

And it may well happen just that way but more likely, and Kubler-Ross came to realize this herself, not necessarily in that order and you may revisit stages more than once.

Some people will stay stuck in one stage through to the end, e.g. Denial. *This is not happening to me. I refuse to accept this diagnosis. I will not give in to death. I'm just not going to die. I don't have time for dying. Just keep giving me more treatments, more drugs, replace more parts, till you find a cure for death... if not, freeze my brain and put it back in another body 50 or 100 years from now when you find a cure for my disease.*

Anger may erupt at any time, during any of the other stages; may even continue up to the end. Anger at God, anger at the doctors, anger at medical science, anger at insurance company decisions, anger at the government, anger at every driver on the road, anger that you have to wait, anger at every phone caller, anger that no one has called you back. There is no end to the anger some people feel about the end of their lives, the unfairness of having to die, of having to deal with a disease process and all the changes that brings into one's life.

If anger doesn't work, you may try to make a deal. You Bargain with God... if you let me live long enough to see my daughter married, until after Christmas, after I get to see my first grandchild, after the Mets win the World Series, then I'll be able to let go. You bargain with your doctors, with your children, with anybody for a few days without pain or physical discomfort, for a little more time to enjoy the summer... anything to postpone the end.

Many religious people may be filled with guilt or shame about something they did, or think they did, to someone else. They may fear they offended God and will be punished or sent to Hell for eternity. And depending on their perception of "hell" that could be pretty fearful. Others suddenly find themselves confronted with their fear of nothingness, oblivion, no life after death. They often spend the time they have left so filled with fear that they fall into a deep Depression and no amount of encouragement will bring them out of it. They die terrified of the unknown.

Some people fall into depression and never come out of it because they are so afraid of death their brain all but shuts down. They can't think. They can't process the medical information, the drug regimen, the treatment schedule. They can't make decisions. They refuse to talk about it. They feel hopeless and helpless, out of control. They may turn it all over to someone else and become completely passive and child-like.

Another underlying issue we're confronted with at the end of life if we've neglected it so far, is our *existential angst* about death. What happens after we die? Is there life after death? Is there a Heaven and a Hell? Is there a Judgment? Is there a "God" we'll have to answer to? Or is it just lights out?

We may have put this conversation with our self off until now, but now it is in our face and we have to deal with it. Much of one's dying time is taken up pondering these questions. People with firm religious convictions are sure they have the answers and have found peace with their understanding of death and what, if anything, happens next. Yet even for these people, Acceptance may still be difficult to reconcile.

Many who claim to have no angst about death and believe that's it — when it's over, it's over, think they have achieved acceptance, but for many of them there is that nagging doubt that keeps popping up now and again... *what if?* They may think they don't have a problem with death... until the moment before they actually die and go into a state of panic as they suddenly see the other side and realize their mistake.

People who are "spiritual but not religious," and there are many varieties of this, often have an easier time moving toward acceptance because they see death, as Dr. Kubler-Ross put it, as simply taking off an old over coat at the end of winter and stepping out into spring.

Those who see death as a transition from one reality to another in full consciousness, as a transformation like the caterpillar becoming a butterfly, see the soul leaving the body and returning home as a light being existing at a higher frequency, have no fear, no hesitation, no remorse... only peace and joyous expectation of their journey home.

Death With Dignity

Some people may choose to exercise their option to hasten their own death rather than have their pain managed beyond their definition of quality of life. It's not a matter of them wanting to die but of wanting an end to their pain and suffering altogether according to their personal definition. Not wanting to experience the end stages of a debilitating disease is not cowardice nor necessarily the symptom of a mental problem.

Aid-in-dying near the end of a long illness is in no way like suicide because a person can no longer cope with their life situation or because of a failed relationship. It's not giving up hope, it is reaching acceptance of what is. Calling dying patients suiciders for wanting to hasten their departure impacts them and their families negatively. It's not accurate and it's not fair.

The intent is not to destroy life but to compassionately end physical suffering and liberate one's soul. It's not done frivolously nor taken lightly; everyone involved is in agreement. The person only does it when the person is ready to let go. It's not done to someone; it's done for those who are ready to transition with peace and dignity on their own terms.

A person requesting aid-in-dying does not have to be depressed or mentally ill to want to exercise this option. For them, continuing to live is not a realistic choice. More likely people who do make a request to exercise their right to death with dignity (DWD) have thought long and hard about it, discussed it with their family and friends, their physician and spiritual advisor, their God or conscience, and come to the conclusion that this is the course that brings them comfort.

One suggestion is to create a list of 100 Things that you do every day from the moment you wake up until you go to sleep at night. When you can no longer do any of these actions, cross them off. This is where you decide when the quality of your life makes it no longer worth continuing to live. Is your cut off point 10 or 3 or 20 or...? You decide when it's time.

Reasonable laws can prevent abuse while honoring self-respect, human dignity and compassion. Just as an obstetrician might administer a drug to hasten a birth, a doctor may prescribe a drug that will hasten not death but the rebirth of our spiritual nature. Prepared ahead of time and guided by a transition guide's voice reading one's Personal Transition Guidebook, it is a peaceful journey home beyond the veil.

Some people believe it is a slippery slope to allow this at all. They postulate mentally or physically disabled or senile elderly people or coma patients will be murdered purely for convenience. Perhaps in some societies where human life isn't valued that could be true. It is up to those who believe in death with dignity to make sure laws are in place to prevent forced euthanasia by designating medical professionals and safe procedures to provide humane, compassionate assistance to those who decide of their own free will to exercise this option.

A May 2005 Gallup Poll indicated that 75% of Americans support "euthanasia" for certain patients but only 58% support "doctor-assisted suicide" for the same patients. Use of the term "suicide" was the only difference in the question asked. The Gallup Poll conclusion was that the use of the word suicide caused the apparent conflict in values.

Opponents count on the negative emotional impact of the term. Calling it "suicide" or "murder" conjures up images that clash with religious beliefs and humanitarian values, but have nothing to do with personal choice at the end of life.

This is what Dr. Jack Kervorkian fought for — a patient's right to choose and the physician's role at end of life. It's nobody's business except the person who is dying, his physician and his family members (and sometimes not the latter). It's continuing care *through* the end of life.

Instead of physicians *abandoning* their patients at the end of their invasive medical treatment options, they could continue to be there for them to provide the medication that will quickly end their suffering if that is their patient's final request.

Their Hippocratic oath says, *firstly, do no harm,* but if forcing a person to stay alive as their body progressively deteriorates for years, whether physically or mentally, isn't doing harm, I don't know what is. Seems to me physicians need a better understanding of compassion. Continuing to swear an oath to Greek gods is out of touch with contemporary reality — the earth is not flat and doctors are not gods.

The American Public Health Association recognizes the profound differences between a typical "suicide" and a terminally ill, mentally competent adult taking life-ending medication if suffering becomes unbearable.

Current medical practice allows patients to choose to withdraw or withhold medical treatment and physicians to prescribe pain medication that sedates the patient into unconsciousness while food and hydration is withheld, thus hastening death. This process is called "terminal sedation," not suicide because the patients are already in the process of dying.

Twenty-some years ago, my step-father, who lived through his first wife's battle with cancer, was determined not to go through what she did when he got cancer. Once his doctors determined no more could be done, he went home, put his affairs in order, filled out his final paperwork, and stopped eating and drinking. Compassion & Choices even has a name for it now, Voluntarily Stop Eating and Drinking (VSED).

Red died peacefully in his own bed with my mother sitting by his side knitting. For some people, this is an easy death; for others, not so easy as it can take a week or more to starve oneself to death and the pain with some diseases can become a lingering, agonizing process.

The next option is enough morphine to keep the person comatose until the body shuts down, which could take many hours, if not days. Yet provided with the proper medication under DWD, death usually comes within a few minutes as the person gently falls asleep.

Death With Dignity laws define a process whereby a

physician, under specific circumstances, may prescribe a medication, usually nembutal or pentobarbital, that will end suffering and hasten transition. This is called aid-in-dying or physician-assisted dying, but currently the physician can only write the prescription. He cannot administer the medication nor be there to help the patient administer or monitor vital signs as the life force leaves the body.

- CompassionAndChoices.org advocates for changes in the law and provides counseling to people who opt to use the law
- FinalExitNetwork.org provides information about state laws, and counseling and information about self-deliverance

Prohibitive and restrictive laws force people, who are determined to end their lives or help a loved one, to take drastic measures, which often produce botched results and worse medical outcomes. Sometimes these measures leave the person in a vegetative state and the loved one accused of attempted murder. This is totally inhumane and contrary to compassion in dying. We treat our animals with greater respect at the end of their lives.

If someone is opposed to death with dignity and would refuse it, that's her choice based on her beliefs. If a person believes there is an afterlife where she is welcomed and loved, and is ready to go home, there shouldn't be a law based on some other group's belief system that condemns such people to hell or makes it illegal for everyone else.

No one should be punished in this life nor will they be in the next for helping someone fulfill her last wishes, as current laws and the Catholic Bishops Conference recently proclaimed. And they have no right to impose their beliefs on the rest of humanity. This isn't a religious issue; it is a personal decision.

Sometimes healing doesn't mean curing the disease but providing a pain-free, peaceful transition, and this requires the participation of caring physicians and spiritual guides. As I mentioned previously, palliative care, which might be able to help a person deal with their pain isn't always available and even a hospice nurse can't guarantee she will be at the bedside if your dying loved one is suffering in the middle of the night.

Being able to have a physician or nurse practitioner, or even a newly created medical specialist, legally available to administer a drug and monitor one's dying process while a transition guide reads the person's Personal Transition Guidebook would be a compassionate ending to this life and rebirthing to the next.

Hopefully it will be considered part of a continuum of services program in the future to assist patients to make a peaceful transition when death of the body is the expected outcome of aging or a disease process if that's how they choose to go.

Thirty-five used to be old, not so long ago. In some countries, it still is. But in the "developed" world, thanks to medical science, people live well into their 80s and 90s and they are dying from diseases people didn't develop because they died younger.

We are in the early stages of an old age population boom and this presents new problems that need to be addressed. If someone is diagnosed with Alzheimer's, will they be eligible for a life-ending prescription they can self-administer should they decide they don't want to go down that road or will they be forced to live it out against their will?

Medical personnel may know what the dying body is going through, what is happening physically. They may have some idea of what the person is going through mentally, whether they are filled with fear, denial, worry, anxiety or are at peace and ready to let go. But rarely do they consider that the person's soul or essence may be hovering above the body observing everything that is being done to it and hearing everything being said, as NDErs are telling us. If they did, healing would take on a whole new meaning.

Perhaps there is a more peaceful way to hasten one's transition at the end of life — one that doesn't involve a pump or a pill or a weapon — or a physician. Perhaps it can all be done in consciousness, with awareness — and we do have free will.

I heard a man say about his deteriorating quality of life that as long as he could still lie in bed, watch football on TV, drink his food through a straw and have his butt wiped, he'd be happy to stay alive by whatever means. For someone like me, that would be way beyond my tolerance.

I believe that when I get to a certain stage whether from old age or illness I will consciously shut down my organs and slip out the top of my head when I'm ready, hug my children and grandchildren one last time, and be off into the Light filled with peace and joy.

I think that anybody who seriously practices this method of conscious dying and is able to shift their consciousness while still in their body will be able to hasten their transition on their own terms without any outside help... but maybe that's just me!

NOTES · NOTES · NOTES · NOTES · NOTES

NOTES · NOTES · NOTES · NOTES · NOTES

Chapter 2

"Just when the caterpillar thought it was over, it became a butterfly."
~ Ancient Proverb

The Art of Conscious Dying

As most contemporary NDErs describe, after leaving their bodies, their consciousness expanded and they became aware they existed in a beautiful world beyond this one. They could still see and hear what was going on in the physical world. They tell of feelings of unconditional love, complete acceptance, overwhelming peace and joy, absolute bliss. They describe their experience as a welcoming homecoming.

It seems that when a physical body dies, conscious awareness of what is going on around it continues almost as if nothing happened, reminiscent of the scene in the movie *Ghost* when Patrick Swayze's character gets shot and he starts running after the gunman. It's not until he comes back to see Demi Moore's character crying over his body that he realizes he is dead and freaks out. This is a good example of dying *un*consciously... unaware that there is no separation between life and death. When the bad guys died, they were completely unaware and overwhelmed by their own negative energy.

If you want to be prepared for your transition journey whenever it happens, no matter how it happens, the modern NDE perspective provides a model for dying consciously — aware of what is happening, what to expect, and enjoying the whole experience. This is especially true in the case of sudden or unexpected death, when there is no time to prepare ahead.

Without this foreknowledge, it would be like going on a trip to a foreign country without a passport, no money, no luggage, no knowledge of the place, no maps, and knowing nothing of the language or customs there. The person is likely to struggle and stumble around when with a little advance preparation for the journey, his cognitive dissonance would be brief.

One may learn this practice now and make it part of one's lifestyle, and the awareness will be there if that unexpected time comes. Or one can wait until told he has six months or less to live because of an illness to prepare himself for a peaceful exit whenever that time comes. The longer one stays in denial there is even the slightest possibility death could result, however, the less time there will be to practice the exercises. A sudden stroke or heart attack may cut that time short.

This experience of dying, which so many people fear is some sort of ending, according to NDE reports, is actually the beginning of an incredibly beautiful, awesome, wondrous adventure in which we get to participate fully. This expansion of our awareness into other dimensions of life offers our soul an amazing opportunity to rise to higher levels of consciousness at transition.

NDErs reveal that
• there is nothing to fear
• the essence of who we are does not die
• "death" refers only to the physical body
• consciousness is continuous

Death is our transformation from our temporary physical form back to our eternal spiritual essence, which is ultimately Oneness with All That Is.

Accordingly, we can prepare ourselves ahead of time no matter what our physical state is, to get the most benefit for our soul growth and development during our transition. By practicing to die before we die, when we do finally leave our body, it will be a completely natural, peaceful experience.

Psychiatrist and near-death experiencer, Carl Jung said that it is psychologically beneficial to have death as a goal toward which to strive.

Mozart called death the key to unlocking the door to true happiness.

Shakespeare wrote that when we are prepared for death, life is sweeter.

Philosopher Michel de Montaigne said "to practice death is to practice freedom."

Dying consciously, with full awareness of what is going on and what to do next, and moving directly into the Light of Unconditional Love, allows us to accelerate our spiritual growth and the evolution of our consciousness. It is the secret to dying well.

We have the sleep of forgetfulness when we transition into the physical world and the clarity of awakened consciousness when we transition back home.

Practicing to Die Before We Die

We have all the information, it just needs to be put into a coherent form (e.g., Personal Transition Guidebook) that makes sense to us and fits seamlessly into our lifestyle. Ancient knowledge has given us a model of the energy system that allows us to exist as human beings (Chakras) and the sequence of the activation and deactivation of the soul's subtle connections to its biological host, which will be explained later. We may use this imagery along with the descriptions of physical symptoms of people as they are dying to visualize what the journey would look like in consciousness. We know more about it now because we have learned to listen to the dying.

The ancient wisdom teachers got this information the same way I did, by having near-death or other mystical experiences, and struggled the same way I do, trying to put it into words that people can relate to. In this book, I'm tying all this information together to make it accessible and understandable to more people.

Those who sit at the bedsides of the dying, like Kubler-Ross did, have told us physical symptoms to watch for and, although no two deaths are alike, there are many similarities. As hospice nurses, Callanan and Kelly, who described deathbed visions, conversations with loved ones on the other side and special moments with their dying hospice patients in their book, say:

> ... *the messages of Nearing Death Awareness provide a framework within which death can cease to be viewed as a lonely, frightening, overpowering event, as well as a setting in which those close to the one dying can foster sources of comfort in the face of death's inevitability.*

In his book about childhood NDEs, Morse described his patients' journeys out of their bodies into the Light and their glimpses into possible afterlife experiences to give us ideas about how, since we do eventually leave our body, we would like our own transition to go. When asked whether NDEs are real or imagined, Dr. Morse wrote:

> *Near-death experiences involve the perception of another reality superimposed over this one. This "other reality" frequently is a spiritual one involving the existence of a loving god. There is clearly a sense of a persistence of consciousness after the death of the body. If near-death experiences are "real" then clearly it is possible that this other reality is real and even our destination after death. Furthermore, if near-death experiences are real, then an entire class of currently trivialized spiritual visions such as after death communications, shared dying experiences, and premonitions of death are most likely also real.*

If your choice would be to die peacefully at home with your loved ones around your bedside, then practicing the art of conscious dying and writing your Personal Transition Guidebook offers you that opportunity.

Deepak Chopra has probably done more to bring eastern and western thought together in his 50-plus books than anyone else. He's shown us how one belief system has been built on another and disclosed the common themes that run through all the myths and stories over thousands of years.

In *Life After Death,* Dr. Chopra draws on cutting edge scientific discoveries and the great wisdom traditions to provide us with a map of the afterlife and concludes that practicing to die before we die is the key to our spiritual growth. He says:

> *Concepts like birth and death, life and death, have no relevance. There is only existence. To be is an all-enveloping experience. It must always be kept in mind that the afterlife is not as "after" as we assume. All three dimensions of consciousness are ever-present space.*

We can practice meditation to relax; use guided imagery to prepare ourselves mentally, emotionally and spiritually to release our attachments to the physical world; forgive what needs forgiveness and express gratitude to those we love; and write our Personal Transition Guidebook about a peaceful, joy-filled journey to the other side based on what we believe to be true.

If we get what we expect, as many NDErs suggest, that will be the beginning of our experience as we leave our body, bid our loved ones goodbye and merge with the Light. We can use the power of our imaginations to describe our desired personal journey.

Cancer survivors or people with gradually debilitating conditions like MS, ALS, or Parkinson's disease may live for many years after diagnosis and treatments. There is plenty of time to practice the recommended exercises, create guided visualizations to help a person work on forgiveness and gratitude, and write one's Personal Transition Guidebook before physical abilities become lost. Once a person has practiced them, they become part of their consciousness.

The goal of those who practice dying consciously while they have the cognitive capacity to do so is to awaken in full consciousness during their transition no matter what condition their body or brain is in at the time of death. Even for those who later develop Alzheimer's, their consciousness will reawaken fully on the other side. Diseases and disabilities are left behind with the physical body and brain. The soul is perfect.

The knowledge that our conscious experience continues after death and that physical death is not an ending but a doorway to a higher state of consciousness where life goes on, offers peace of mind at the end of this life. Realization that the departure of a loved one from her earthly body means a celebrated reunion with her spiritual family on the other side helps us achieve acceptance in our grief over losing her physical presence in this lifetime.

Knowing we will join again with those loved ones who made their transition before us and those who will come after us, frees us to live this lifetime to the fullest guided by Love and Compassion.

A transition guide, whether a professional or family caregiver, teaches others how to integrate the relaxation exercise into their daily wellness regimen and to use guided visualization to do their inner growth work, which will prepare them for a peaceful transition whenever and however it happens.

In the meantime as they practice how to die before their body dies, they will discover the peace of mind they may have been missing in this life. The hardest part is getting people to talk about their own death.

The Process of Transition

If we're all going to experience dying, and if we don't get complete choice in the circumstances of that dying, wouldn't it be a good idea to figure out what parts we do have choice over, and use those parts as grace-fully as possible?
~ Patricia A Webb
David's Passage: Stories of Conscious Dying

Sudden Death

Death may come without warning or there may be an instant before death that the person realizes her death is inevitable — an automobile accident, falling off a cliff, being murdered, drowning. Some will experience sheer terror, some a moment of great peace, after which they will find themselves awake on the other side of a very thin veil looking at their dead body and wondering what all the fuss is about because they feel just fine.

Those who approach death filled with fear may linger around their body, still confused, frightened, angry, not believing or accepting that they are dead. They may be unwilling to let go even though their loved ones on the other side may be urging them to cross over — to come home. They may be unable to let go of their attachments to the physical world, unsure about what comes next and what, if anything, they can do.

The moment they recognize their loved ones and their Spiritual Transition Guide on the other side, who are waiting to help them heal their soul and put their whole life into perspective, their joy-filled journey will begin. Otherwise they may resist going into the Light, continue to deny they died, and just hang around wondering what the heck just happened and why everyone seems to be ignoring them.

Those who have previously worked with a transition guide and die suddenly, unexpectedly, are prepared for death whenever it comes. They don't linger around their physical body wondering what happened. They won't refuse to leave the vicinity of their body because they are immediately aware that their body has ceased to function and they are no longer connected to it; no longer have need of it. There is no shock or fear or confusion. They know to go immediately toward the Light to complete their transition back to their spiritual home.

If a person has worked through her life review process and changed from a material to a spiritual life path before death, she will get back to her existence on the other side quickly.

If she started her life review process while still in body but was still working on it when death came, she will at least be prepared by knowing how to move through the early part of her transition relatively quickly, work through the remainder of her earthly issues more easily during her life review on the other side, and return more seamlessly to her spiritual family.

The goal is to become conscious of our selves as spiritual beings while we exist in human form, before our human body dies. This evolution in consciousness is our collective spiritual journey, as well as each individual's spiritual journey. As spiritual guru Andrew Cohen said:

Evolution is a cosmic process that is going somewhere in and through time. And we are all part of that process. This simple fact is potentially life transforming, but it's also hard to grasp at a deep level. The process that created us is moving. We tend to see the world around us as static. But it's not. It's going somewhere. We're going somewhere. Awakening to this truth about all of manifestation changes the way we see the world around us and our place in it. The biggest and most important part of this awakening is that we discover our power to affect where the process that created us is going. We realize the ultimate reason for our own existence: to be a spiritual hero, to boldly take responsibility for the future of the process itself.

Lingering Death

At a hospice seminar I attended years ago, the speaker asked the audience if they would rather experience sudden death or a lingering death. Most people raised their hands for sudden death so they wouldn't have to deal with anything and it would just be over. Then she went on to tell us that hospice patients talk about how happy they are that they got to:

- Spend the time they had left wrapping up their lives
- Take care of unfinished business
- Say goodbye to family and friends

- Say what needed to be said
- Forgive and to ask for forgiveness
- Set things right
- Work on their Bucket List
- Write or record an oral history to leave to the family
- Organize family photo albums
- Go through their possessions and give them away to their loved ones with time to see them enjoy their gifts
- Plan their own funerals
- Arrange to have a going away party with all their friends and family gathered around them one last time
- Invite loved ones to be at their bedside when they crossed over

When these people were ready to begin to let go, it was because they were at peace with themselves, their lives, and the end of their lives on earth. Death can then be looked at as a rite of passage, a graduation, a celebration of a life well lived — it is no longer a tragic ending when we know we don't die — we simply leave the room assured that we will all be together again on the other side.

Enlightened people, those who already realize we are all spiritual beings having human experiences and everyone is somewhere along their eternal spiritual path, understand that death is simply the doorway to the other side. There is no-*thing* to fear.

Death is simply a transformation from one state and form of energy/being to another, where we re-organize our atoms and pick up where we left off before choosing to live another lifetime as a human personality. The caterpillar becoming a butterfly pales in comparison to the magnificence of our transfiguration from a physical to a spiritual being.

As a hospice volunteer for many years, I realized doing everything may not always be the best choice and a lingering death isn't necessarily a painful death, although with certain illnesses, it can be extremely painful. When medical science has nothing more to offer to help a human body overcome aging or a disease process, or a person decides not to accept further medical treatment, hospice allows persons nearing the end of this life to be as pain-free as possible while their physical body is shutting down.

However, there is no one there to help a dying person prepare herself mentally, emotionally and spiritually leading up to her transition, which is where transition guides come in. Not to replace one's priest or the hospice chaplain, but to enhance their support. Some people have a strong belief system and approach death confidently, but even some of those may be fearful, anxious, scared, looking for someone who understands what they are going through, not just offering platitudes.

How did you answer that question about sudden or lingering death? If your first response was sudden death, you now may want to reconsider your preference. Families often express gratitude to hospice for having been privileged to have those last few peaceful months at home with their loved ones. People who experience the death of a loved one in ICU, especially involving having to make the decision to turn off life support machines, are often traumatized for years.

Nearing Death Awareness

People who are approaching death may begin to retreat more into their inner world where they start to mentally prepare themselves for transition. They become less concerned with the comings and goings on in the physical world. Please don't read a newspaper aloud or have TV/radio news on around a dying person unless they specifically request it. It's really not the last thing they need to be hearing as they lay dying.

They may eat less and sleep more, spend more time lying in bed, contented, in a dream-like state. Their excretory functions will slow down. They may be restless or agitated depending on their pain level. Their complexion and skin tone will change. They have less need to communicate with others. They may prefer to be alone, to not talk about trivial matters or healthcare concerns, to stare off into space and talk to them selves (more likely they are communicating with their deceased loved ones). They have entered the stage hospice nurses Callanan and Kelley called "nearing death awareness."

As death nears, a person may sound more and more congested, there may be a rattling sound in their throat. Their breathing patterns will slow. Their blood pressure and pulse will lower. They may drift in and out of consciousness or seem to be in a coma for long periods of time then suddenly awaken and be lucid, only to drop off again. They may call out to dead relatives or try to describe what they are seeing.

Whether prepared to die or not, the dying one will be quite busy sorting things out on some level of consciousness, but she may be confused and frightened if she doesn't know what to expect, if she hasn't prepared herself for this time between the ending of physical life and spiritual rebirth.

Some people may become very agitated, restless or confused about what is happening inside and around them. They are not likely to be able to communicate what they are experiencing. This can be unsettling to those at the bedside who also don't understand what is happening to their loved one. The current hospice response is likely to be — *give her more morphine.*

Physician-Assisted Dying

Previous sections have dealt with a process of dying during which we have very little control. We can't predict when it will happen, where we will be when it does, or whether it will be quick or interminable, painful and torturous or peaceful and serene.

Most people would say they want to die at home in their own bed in their sleep but these days our caregivers are more likely to panic and call 9-1-1, and will be resuscitated, tubed, lined, paralyzed, and kept alive on a respirator in an ICU... several times before our heart just can't take anymore.

Now with increased palliative care, pain management, and hospice care, many people choose to stop medical treatments at some point and go home to wrap up their lives and spend time with their family. There is time to work with a transition guide, to reconcile one's life and practice guided visualizations to prepare themselves for their journey home.

In some cases, with some medical conditions and disease processes, the pain is so great or the quality of life can become so unbearable or there is no let up from suffering, the person might consider the option offered by the Death With Dignity Act currently available to terminally ill patients in Oregon, Washington, Vermont and New Mexico. The Montana Supreme Court found nothing indicating that physician aid in dying is against public policy, but has not yet passed a law protecting physicians from prosecution.

Similar laws are currently being debated in half a dozen other states, including Colorado, Connecticut, Massachusetts, Nevada, New Hampshire, New Jersey, and Pennsylvania. Generally, the laws allow patients with a terminal condition and a prognosis of six months or less to live to request a prescription from a medical doctor for enough of a medication to allow the patient to put himself to sleep when and if he chooses to do so.

People who choose this option may plan their dying experience as a special occasion, a family healing time. Using the information and practices in this book could help make this a beautiful experience of sharing love and memories as the family says goodbye to their loved one and sends them off peacefully on their journey home — rather than a fearful, frightening, traumatic experience for all concerned.

The dying person's Transition Guidebook can be read as a family affair and treasured as a family tradition. The person's religious beliefs may be incorporated into this new family ritual, assisting family members as they move on.

On the day of his choice, with all family members present, the departing person raises his cup with the others in a final toast, lies back and gently falls into a peaceful sleep. As he does, his consciousness rises out of his body and up to the ceiling, usually in a corner of the room at first. He will "see" the scene around his bedside and the realization that he is no longer in his body will come to him.

Knowing that he can, because he prepared himself for this, he will surround each of his loved ones with his love and gratitude, and then he will embark on his journey home.

The Transfiguration

The death of the body involves the shutting down of organs and the nervous system. The heart stops pumping blood to the brain and the brain cells die. Extremities turn blue and blood pools on the underside of the body. The body becomes lifeless. All observable activities cease. Decomposition begins as cells die.

What cannot be observed or monitored (yet) is the withdrawal of the life force and consciousness from the physical body, which frees the spiritual body to rise above. In a sense, we shed our skin, like a snake. While conscious awareness is shifting from physical to spiritual, the soul is in the process of withdrawing its connections to the body and preparing for rebirth into the spiritual world.

Just as the placenta, the cord that carries life-giving blood from the mother to the developing fetus, is severed after birth, the etheric cord that carries the life force between the soul and its human form withdraws and is severed after death.

According to Ancient Mystery School teachings (e.g., Astara.org, Rosicrucian.org), the soul gradually deposits three permanent seed atoms into the developing fetus via this etheric cord. These seed atoms make up who we are and carry our DNA sequencing (our life plan). The first implants in the heart and causes it to begin beating.

Several months later the next seed atom implants in the solar plexus area (liver) awakening feelings and at the moment of birth the third awakens consciousness by implanting in the pineal gland in the center of the brain (Third Eye). These three points are involved in the Chakra system of energy that connects the physical body to the etheric energy field that surrounds us. More about Chakras in Chapter 3.

During the transition process, the emotional atom is the first to detach as the person loses interest in every day aspects of the physical world. As the physical brain shuts down, the mental atom is released and all thoughts and concerns about the physical world cease. Conscious awareness however continues with the soul. At physical death, the heart atom is released and the etheric cord begins to withdraw.

It may take several hours to several days for the etheric cord to detach completely and for this reason it's been suggested that cremation or burial not take place until three days after death though religious practices and personal preferences should always be respected.

With a sudden death, the mental and emotional atoms may withdraw simultaneously or within a few minutes of each other although it may take some time for the heart atom and the etheric cord to detach. This may explain why some people may be resuscitated or regain consciousness on their own.

All of those people nearly die and may have an OOBE, but only some of those have a "core" NDE. If the mental and emotional atoms do not return after resuscitation, the human being remains in a comatose state, or may be mentally or emotionally compromised.

If the etheric cord is severed, the life force is withdrawn and resuscitation is not possible. A body may be kept "alive" artificially on ventilators, but it is not revivable as a conscious being. Consciousness has transformed into a diaphanous Being of Light ready to return to Source and continue on its journey home.

The Role of a Transition Guide

A transition guide is somewhat of a personal assistant for people who desire to prepare themselves ahead of time for a better dying experience. They are teacher, counselor, problem solver, witness, confessor, companion, coach, minister, healer, researcher, nurse. They will walk you through it and talk you through it, and guide you to the Light by helping you prepare and by reading your Personal Transition Guidebook. That being said, every relationship will be different depending on the people involved and the circumstances.

Above all there has to be a bond of trust between the dying person and her transition guide as this can be an extremely intimate relationship. Transition guides are encouraged to practice detachment so as not to become emotionally involved with their clients; to empathize, not sympathize; to be compassionate in all circumstances.

In some cases, it may be easier for a person planning their exit strategy to be more open with a stranger who is a professional transition guide than an emotionally involved family member.

As my friend Kelsey Collins, who advocates for the elderly, states in her book *Exit Strategy:*

Our elders don't want our pity; they want our precious time and they want it consistently. They want to be heard, just like every other human being, and they want to feel valuable, just like you and I do.

The person who is learning these techniques needs to be open-minded and willing to practice on her own so these tools will become useful to her more quickly when she needs them. Continuing to think there will be time later if one is already on a disease path can lead to bewilderment and confusion if one takes a sudden turn for the worse. In some cases, it could be too late to begin the practice.

With the support of a transition guide, the person who is practicing to die consciously learns to enter her inner world during guided visualization sessions. She may be seeing herself as she really is (often for the very first time) and learning how she might have shown more compassion, love and kindness during the lifetime she is preparing to leave. She may be learning what had been her soul's mission in this life (often for the first time) and reviewing what she accomplished and failed to accomplish in that regard.

She may want to make last minute amends to certain people in her life. The transition guide may be able to facilitate this by contacting family members and encouraging communication. If a referee is needed, better to hire a professional mediator.

Closer to the day of death, the dying person may be making conscious sojourns to the other side for longer periods of time. She may be recognizing deceased relatives, close friends, religious figures or spiritual beings, and may call out to them or tell others about them upon returning to this reality.

The transition guide can encourage her to describe what she sees and discourage others from patronizing her. Just because other people can't see them doesn't mean nothing is there or that the dying person doesn't see something others can't see.

The dying often experience shifts in consciousness prior to death, as if they are moving back and forth from here to there. To those around the bedside, it may appear that their loved one is talking nonsense or gibberish.

It is usually comforting to the dying person to see her loved ones on the other side waiting to greet her, just as she hoped they would be. If the people who witness these deathbed visions were more aware and supportive during this process instead of dismissing them as hallucinations, it would be more helpful to the person.

The dying may be aware of themselves in their bed, surrounded by their children and grandchildren, then be suddenly aware of themselves floating out of their body, above their body, seeing their parents and grandparents waiting for them on the other side of a thinning veil.

They may come back into their body still talking to those on the other side. They may meet a loved one who recently died without their knowing and tell those at the bedside upon returning to physical awareness that they saw them waving from the other side.

They may try to tell those on this side what they are seeing on the other side but can hardly find the words to express their amazement at what they see and feel — and those on this side assume their delirious loved one is seeing things that aren't there and talking crazy.

If the images are evoking fear in the dying person, the transition guide can be a reassuring presence explaining that these are mental images, products of their own thinking, which cannot harm them. Using guided visualization techniques, the images can be changed into pleasant images that can be surrounded by white light or captured in a bubble and floated away.

Listen to what they are saying — these may be the most powerful conversations you will ever have with another human being.

These pre-death visions of the afterlife prepare the dying person to cross over without fear and a transition guide may help ease the tension among family members at the bedside by reading the Personal Transition Guidebook aloud and encouraging their participation.

Some dying people have days of drifting back and forth, and of being able to tell those around them about the wonders they are experiencing, even predicting when they will die, which is a profound experience for those at the bedside to witness — and contributes to the spiritual growth and development of all involved.

The family transition guide helps the family members participate in the dying process of their loved one by keeping the lines of communication open and by being a good listener. People need reassurance about what is happening, if the person is suffering, how long it will take, if anything else that can be done, and so on.

As a transition guide, even if you don't understand or believe that the person is seeing loved ones on the other side, accept what they've said as their truth and allow them space to explore their visions. Encourage them to talk about it, don't rush to request more drugs to shut them up.

Transition guides need to learn the language of the dying. A person may say she is going to depart on a certain day or after some event, and she does so. She may say she wants to go home but not mean the place she last lived. Some may use metaphors or poetry to let others know they will be leaving soon (e.g., the bus is coming, the sun is setting, the curtain is falling). They may say that God or maybe a deceased relative told them it is time.

Some may wait until everyone is out of the room so no one will see them die; others until a certain person arrives to say goodbye before letting go. This indicates we have some awareness of and control over our dying process depending on the circumstances and one's level of awareness.

Our sense of hearing is the last to go as we are dying and becomes telepathic during separation. It is a good time for the transition guide to offer words of encouragement about moving toward the Light. It is not a good time for the dying person to hear crying, wailing, emotional outbursts, or family arguments about medical decisions, funeral arrangements or the Will.

The transition guide may have to diplomatically ask people to leave the room. This not only distracts the person from her journey, but also may keep her from moving into the Light at the earliest opportunity. As telepathic hearing continues for some time after physical death, prayers and readings by the transition guide for the well being of her soul on its journey to the other side will keep her consciously on course.

Hearing the reading she has practiced with her transition guide during her actual transition keeps the dying person focused on letting go on a conscious level so the person does not feel helpless or alone. She will more likely be able to describe her experiences to those at her bedside as she drifts back and forth between worlds. She will be able to maintain her focus because she knows what to expect at the moment of the death of her body and the awakening of pure consciousness.

The last thoughts a person has before her body dies are important to the transition experience and the transition guide will be there to remind her to be thinking about becoming One with her understanding of the Light, God, Ultimate Reality, Source, during her last breaths, as she withdraws from her physical body in full consciousness.

You can see how it would be helpful to one's soul path if one would remember to scream "Oh, my God!" instead of "Oh, *Bleep!*" if one gets hit by that bus.

Communicating with the Dying

When communicating with people who are terminally ill or dying — be honest and straightforward, don't beat around the bush or sugarcoat or patronize or preach. Listen, then follow their lead. They may talk in metaphors about going on a journey or returning home. Repeat what you hear and let them come around to really talking about their concerns and fears.

Suggestions in this book will give you enough background to cover most subjects that might come up. Remember though, it's more important to be a good listener than to be the person with all the answers. It is OK to say, *I don't know... but what do you think?*

In the *Appendix* is a list of the kinds of questions to ask your self to help you sort out your own belief system or for a transition guide to initiate family discussions about values. These same kinds of questions can be asked of the dying person to help her put her own life and death in perspective.

Some people have never really asked themselves these kinds of questions, much less talked about them with family members. They may be used in an exercise to get people to deal with these issues, and to talk about death and dying among their friends and family.

Some people accept that they are dying by just a knowingness that comes over them or may say, *I talked to God and it's OK.* It's those left behind that can have the harder time with acceptance of death and letting go when they feel so much has been left unsaid. It could be helpful to all of them to be included in these kinds of end of life conversations, which the transition guide may initiate to bring healing to the dying person and his family in the last days of his life.

Letting Go

It's written in many ancient texts, including the Bible, and spoken by many philosophers in various ways that we are not our emotions, we are not our intellect, we are not our wealth, we are not our appearance, we are not our body — that we are in the world, but not of it — that we are spiritual beings having human experiences, not the other way around. We are spirits who manifest form in the physical world, not bodies that have a soul. The spark of life inside us is who we truly are; the human body is what we project into the physical world to experience it. It is the coat of skin we wear to be able to function in a physical dimension. But many people don't get that — yet.

Understanding this is in itself a leap of consciousness, a step outside the box you may have been conditioned to believe protects you. Once you get this, you can embrace a holistic worldview that is no longer confined or limited to the physical world. This is the evolution of consciousness. This is what happens to us when we are dying. We begin to see through the veil into another frequency of light, another dimension of All That Is that has always been there just beyond the range of our visual spectrum. This is what hospice nurses tell us their dying patients are telling them. A hospice patient shortly before transitioning asked out loud, "Where did all those angels come from?" Why wait until you are dying to be able to see this for yourself? You can explore your inner realms by learning this simple method of meditation and visualization to practice dying consciously before it is your time to transition. The healthier you are when you start, the better time to begin your practice.

With sudden death, there is no time to let go of those things you thought were important, which on the other side you will realize were not. You will experience a life review where you will see times in your life when you hurt others or yourself, when opportunities to offer forgiveness or express gratitude were missed or taken, times when you were compassionate and times when you could have been more so.

Your addictions to physical things like money, drugs, sex, shopping, food, shoes, including your human life and your loved ones, will keep you from being able to raise your vibrations much above the physical dimension. If you are unable to let go of them, your soul may have to reincarnate quickly without spending much time in the spiritual dimension.

Moderating your lifestyle, becoming kinder, more loving, more compassionate toward all sentient beings, and globally and environmentally conscious during your physical lifetime, may mean less healing energy work needs to be done after transition of consciousness from the body.

We never know when death may come and if it is a sudden death it can create confusion for the departed soul who hasn't done the work before this moment.

It isn't about judgment or sin, or what church you attend or whether you accept this religion or that. It isn't about how much money you make or how many toys you have or how powerful you are. It isn't about how beautiful you are or what you accumulated. It's more about how kind you were to others, how loving you were. It's that simple. It affects your energy while in a body and it stays with your consciousness when it leaves the body. You experience it in your life review.

If you have a progressive disease that could potentially cause your death over time, learning to practice the art of conscious dying will not only bring you comfort when you are nearing death awareness, but it will bring you peace during treatments, surgeries, and periods of recovery, and it can improve the quality of your life.

By letting go of your emotional *attachments* to physical things and desires, you free yourself from the hold they have on your attention. If you get anxious at the thought of losing something, you are attached to it. When you drop the attachment, you are free to have the thing or not.

A technique for letting go of attachments is to first identify it and then think about what it has cost you in terms of time and money and relationships. Next, feel appreciation for the attachment and what you have gained from it. Then see the attachment leaving you by imagining you put it in a beautiful sailboat and it sails away, or you see it dissolve away in a sparkle of lights, or you reduce it to a tiny speck of light that you place in your heart. Every time the thought arises, return to your image to reinforce your desire to let it go.

It's not woo-woo! Rituals, symbols and myths have been used throughout human history to shift one's consciousness to a higher state of awareness — from attachment to acceptance.

Letting go allows you to live in the present moment and deal with what is happening now. Not the past, not the future, just this moment. In this moment, you can be peaceful. You don't have to be dying to want to feel this inner peace, but you do have to make it a practice to maintain it so it will be there for you throughout your life and when you make your transition.

Another method for letting go and accepting your spiritual nature is through prayer and meditation. When you pray, you are talking to God. When you meditate and become centered, and reach a place of silence in your mind, you are listening to the Wisdom of the Universe, having a conversation with God.

When our "ego" (the part of us that thinks it's separate, alone and in control) nods off (from boredom), we have a clear channel to our own higher wisdom. When our mental chatter ceases to matter and our body feels weightless and unfettered, we can focus on parting the veil and seeing our self as we truly are — a great and wondrous spiritual being living another precious lifetime in a human body.

This is what we realize as our body is dying, as NDErs describe, and which we can all practice before we leave our body. The gift for doing so may be living with inner peace and dying with peace of mind surrounded by Unconditional Love.

Some dying people continue to hang on. Some people have a lot of unfinished business to deal with (karma). Some people just need permission to let go.

Letting go is not the same as giving up. With the latter there is fear and a resignation that life is over or not worth living; with the former it is looking forward to Liberation and Freedom, and a welcome home by our family on the other side.

A dying person who has learned the art of conscious dying already knows he has permission to let go of his physical body and has no need to linger. He may have memorized the words in his Personal Transition Guidebook and may even hasten his transition by his conscious participation in the process. It can also be valuable to those who choose to use the death with dignity option.

Once you have accepted you are preparing for your transition, you are free to participate in it. If you are dying, there is nothing else you need to be doing. Understanding that you are a spiritual being getting ready to slip out of your physical body, and return to your spiritual form and environment, requires just being. You are letting go of who you thought you were and everything connected to that illusion — and recognizing your Divinity.

The closer you get to transition, the less concerned you will be for matters of the physical world. Your attention will be on merging with the Clear Light, seeing God or Allah, experiencing a down pouring of grace, meeting Jesus or Buddha, or seeing your loved ones because you have prepared yourself for this sacred adventure and know something about what to expect.

You create your own experience with your thoughts. What you think about, you will manifest and where your mind dwells mostly during your life and at the moment of death will be reflected in your transitional journey home. If you die in fear, anger, bitterness, guilt or shame that will be part of your experience. If you die surrounding yourself with love and light that will be the overall tone of your experience. When I talk about raising your consciousness or raising your vibration to a higher frequency, this is what I'm talking about.

You can begin to do this work before you leave your body so you can go directly into the Light when you awaken, fully conscious, on the other side, looking back into the physical world with a greater sense of appreciation and understanding as it fades away. One can begin to do this inner work any time in life. As you lie dying or suddenly find yourself out of your body, it will bring you comfort as you review your life.

Acceptance of Death and Dying

Dr. Kubler-Ross talks about acceptance being the final stage of loss or grief. It's not a resignation but a sense of empowerment. Some people will fight for life up until their last breath, but many naturally reach a point of acceptance in the days or weeks before, and begin to prepare themselves for their dying time. The fighting is from fear of annihilation, fear that dead is dead, the end, nothingness.

It can be quite difficult to even get into a conversation with a person with this belief system. Others may ask tentative questions to test your reaction and when they find they can trust you, they will open up and want to know more about making a peaceful transition, and being consciously aware of what's going on as they do.

It becomes part of these end of life conversations you will have while practicing the relaxation exercises and guided journeys, doing forgiveness and gratitude exercises, conducting a life review, and writing one's Personal Transition Guidebook. For people who have trouble verbalizing their deepest thoughts, journaling may be a good way to get them to open up, and start sorting out and coming to terms with their lives.

It's important for transition guides, especially those who do this companioning work with people other than an immediate family member, to have already dealt with the grief and loss issues in their own lives through counseling and other grief work. It's important to reach acceptance of the inevitability of our own death by doing this inner work ourselves before we can be effective at helping others reach acceptance along their personal path to wholeness.

Preparing for Transition

The dying person may be able to express preferences of her own or be open to suggestions about her environment. She may want to arrange to die in her own home, surrounded by her loved ones, but this isn't always possible. If she is hospitalized or resides in a hospice or assisted living home, the transition guide may still be able to arrange for some of the following suggestions if the staff is open to new ideas.

These are just suggestions — ideas garnered from reading about different religious and ritual practices around the world and throughout human history. It is completely up to the dying person to make decisions like these. A transition guide is there to support all her last wishes and final arrangements.

Room Arrangements

There are no precedents about *deathing* rooms so it is open to one's creativity. If the person is in an ICU or nursing home, there may be some restrictions; however, at one's own home there are endless possibilities for the imagination. Anything from a sacred ceremonial circle to a replica of your childhood bedroom; a picture window with a beautiful view with bird feeders, and flowers and trees to watch as the seasons change.

Make the room bright and cheerful, filled with happy memories. If candles and incense (preferably mild, like Sandalwood) are desired and not prohibited (as they might be in a hospital), they may be placed in the room.

Keep the lighting dim, a white unscented candle might be sufficient, keep talking to a minimum. Doors and windows may be closed to maintain silence, especially if in a noisy environment, like a hospital or nursing home. Turn off phones, cell phones, and other electronics that beep or chime or play loud music.

Light/Color

An orange light or the color orange stimulates the head centers. The life force will exit the body at the Chakra most habitually expressed during life, but it will be attracted to orange and it is possible that a person may experience spiritual illumination for the first time while still in body if their energy can reach the Crown Chakra — which means the dying person gets a momentary glimpse beyond the veil prior to death and may even be able to express what they see.

Oh Wow! Oh Wow! Oh Wow!
~Steve Jobs

Music

Mantras or chanting, soothing classical or New Age music, harp or flute music, religious music, may be desirable in the earlier stages of the dying process. At some point music or chanting may be more of a distraction and you may have to rely on your intuition about turning it down or off. During the transition process, there are sounds (celestial sounds, music of the spheres, a chorus of angels) or the Sound of Silence the departing soul may be listening to.

There are some musicians who have had NDEs who attempt to reproduce the sounds they heard during their experience through their instruments. Others, music thanatologists, play live harp or flute at the bedside for those who are nearing their transition. This may also appeal to a person who is practicing conscious dying before actually nearing death awareness.

Personal Objects

The dying person may want to arrange to have things meaningful to her placed around her bedside — family pictures, personal objects, flowers, religious symbols, etc. Some people may spend a lot of time lying in bed staring at the walls and ceiling. It makes sense for there to be meaningful images around for her to look at rather than a blank wall.

Photos will help her with her life review, much of which she may do non-verbally. Religious objects, pictures, symbols familiar to her may keep her focused on going into the Light. Having her favorite pet beside her may be comforting.

Preparing an Effigy

In case the person's death occurs away from home or

when the transition guide isn't available, a photo and several personal objects/religious symbols may be used in place of the body to focus on while their transition guide reads their Guidebook.

The departing soul will be able to tune in to the familiar voice no matter the distance between them. Depending on the arrangements, the transition guide may want to ask for these objects early on in the relationship.

Relatives and Friends at the Bedside
The dying person may want to have his loved ones around him while he is making his transition, but they should be advised of his arrangements and his desire to die in full consciousness. The transition guide should discuss these issues with the family beforehand.

Those who are likely to have an outburst of emotion or get into a family argument while a person is dying, should be escorted to another room so they may express themselves where he will not be distracted during his transition process.

As to a person's decision about being present at the side of a dying loved one, no one can understand the true spiritual experience of the sacred journey until he experiences it himself but, regardless of one's personal beliefs, it may be to the dying person's benefit if loved ones can be there for him at this time.

Relatives attending should be asked to direct their mental energies toward helping the dying person recognize the Light and move into it — either by joining with the reader or repeating religious prayers or scriptures the dying person selected; however, noise should be kept to a minimum so the departing consciousness can hear words from his Guidebook being read and concentrate on listening for the Sounds of Silence.

Physical Contact

For the most part we've been conditioned to keep our hands off other people, particularly the elderly and the dying. Doctors are notoriously standoffish when it comes to that. They think of people as bodies with a disease or illness that needs to be treated and if medical science fails them, they drop out and move on.

Actually physicians need some of this transition guide training to teach them about compassion and human dignity at the time of death. It might be helpful to the family if the doctor participated in any dying ritual, especially if it's taking place in a hospital. Hospitals have comfortable, homey birthing rooms, why not comfortable, homey deathing rooms?

As a transition guide, it's acceptable with permission to sit on the edge of the patient's bed, hold her hand, hold her in a loving embrace, cry with her, and the family should be encouraged to do the same. If the person wants to be held as she is dying, that's acceptable.

Physical contact may be a distraction to some people, but others may be comforted by it. Just because someone is skin and bones, and curled up in a fetal position doesn't mean they don't need to be held or stroked and treated with kindness.

Home health aides and nursing home aides need this kind of training to teach them to respect the needs of their elderly and dying patients so they don't treat them as if they have no awareness about what's going on around them.

This is a very personal service you will be offering to teach other people. Being warm, friendly, sincere and compassionate will make you a welcome member of the dying person's inner circle.

Granting Last Wishes

A dying patient may reveal to the transition guide a last request that he knows his doctor or family members might disapprove of, and the transition guide may do her best to fulfill it. If he wants a good stiff drink or a glass of his favorite wine, if he wants one last puff of a cigarette, a cigar or a joint, let him have it (make sure there aren't any oxygen tanks in the room before he lights up!). Timothy Leary entered his transition on LSD. How can it hurt? You have to maintain a sense of humor in these situations.

A person may have a Bucket List — a list of things he wants to do or see before he dies. The family may not be so willing to help for various reasons or there may be no family members around. The person may not even want to involve his family. The transition guide can be discreet and find ways to help the person complete his list before he becomes unable to do so on his own.

If a dying person wants to talk about aid-in-dying, use your listening skills to find out what is going on with him that he brings it up. Often times the person may just need more pain medication or personal attention to be comfortable. However, if the person is coherent and determined, and you are comfortable, you may be able to facilitate a family discussion.

You could ask for end of life counseling from

CompassionandChoices.org or FinalExitNetwork.org. You could still be with the person to read his Personal Transition Guidebook as he is dying, but administering the drug or helping the person administer are out of bounds until the laws change. The person has to be able to self-administer. Stay within the boundaries of the law to protect yourself. See current U.S. Death With Dignity laws in the *Appendix*.

Caring for the Caregiver

*To take good care of your self and to take good care of
living beings and the environment is the
best way to love God.*
~ Thich Nhat Hanh

The intensity of concentration one puts into time spent with a dying person and her family, whether it be teaching all of them the process of conscious dying, or reading the Personal Transition Guidebook as their loved one is dying is exhausting — physically, mentally and emotionally draining. Transition guides, especially those who work with many patients, need to recharge their spiritual batteries frequently and to develop a support system to avoid burnout.

Get a massage, do acupuncture, reiki, have energy work done frequently. Go on a spiritual retreat, climb a mountain, get out on the water. Take up Tai Chi, horseback riding, or ballroom dancing; definitely exercise, and be mindful of what you eat and drink. Meditate often. Walk barefoot amid nature more. Write in your journal every day. Pray. Chant. Chill.

Take care of your own body-mind-spirit so you can
continue to enjoy helping others while you are here. If
you are also a caregiver, find a support group through
your local hospice or start one yourself. Above all, don't
try to do it all yourself and don't isolate yourself. To avoid
caregiver burnout, enlist the help of family, friends and
neighbors to put together a transition team that covers
24-7 care.

Grief & Mourning

Grief implies loss and we grieve over the loss of many
things from our innocence to our physical lives. Life
is actually a continuous process of loss as everything
changes and nothing stays the same. All of us grieve in
one way or another about what we've lost in the past or
might lose in the future. As we grow older, we come to
accept some of these losses, even take them in stride.
Some we never get over.

When we lose our money or our job or our health or our
spouse leaves us, we grieve and struggle to put our lives
back together. We may say "what doesn't kill us makes
us stronger," but when it comes to our lives and the lives
of our loved ones, that loss becomes unacceptable. How
do we find a place for that in our hearts and minds? How
do we go on after a loved one dies? We are left with an
empty hole in our hearts that is a permanent record of
our loss.

Culturally, some people outwardly mourn with
wailing and crying or demonstrating the unfairness of it
all by seeking revenge and retribution; others go within,
close themselves off for weeks or months or years from

the rest of the world. What we don't understand, we wrap in rituals to appease whatever angry gods we imagine or our own inner demons. *Why is this happening to me? Why is God punishing me? How could God take my child?*

We attribute to an outside power what we don't understand, what we can't control, what we can't see. Without the awareness that we are all part of a continuous cycle of life and rebirth, and we are always together, just at times in different forms or dimensions, we can't grasp the reality that there is no separation.

As my friend and Transition Guide Terri Daniel, whose son transitioned a few years ago at age 16 following a long degenerative illness and continues to communicate with her today, wrote in their book, *Embracing Death:*

The ego sees itself as the center of the universe, and works tirelessly to maintain its illusion of control and separateness. When great trauma or loss occurs, there's a disruption in that system, and the ego fights frantically to survive and return to the status quo. Every time this happens, we have the opportunity to change our perceptions, move beyond the ego to a higher understanding and align more fully with the Divine. When tragedies can be recognized as opportunities, our experience on earth is much less difficult and much less ruled by fear and panic. Whenever we need a reminder of this, we'll experience a tragedy or loss that stops the ego in its tracks and gives us a chance to listen to the soul instead. This is the whole purpose of incarnation... to remember that we're not separate from each other and not separate from God.

So that empty hole in our hearts I mentioned earlier is not a hole at all but a space for our loved one to always be with us to remind us to watch out for that bus! They haven't left us, we haven't lost them; we just have to communicate with them in a different way — not from a place of grief and loss but in a loving way, from our open heart. Those we lose on this side become our greatest teachers from the other side. Sometimes we just need to be quiet long enough to hear their messages.

I have a picture of my sister Bobbie and me on the wall above my desk, two aspiring young ballerinas dressed in our pink tutus, in a ballet pose each holding a rose, taken a few weeks before she moved beyond the veil. We don't need cell phones to communicate!

NOTES · NOTES · NOTES · NOTES · NOTES

NOTES · NOTES · NOTES · NOTES · NOTES

Chapter 3

"When you do things from your soul, you feel a river moving through you."

~ Rumi

Elements of the Practice

A transition guide will first need to teach the dying person to achieve a relaxed state of body and mind in which to practice conscious dying. You can call this a meditation or self-hypnosis or simply a relaxation exercise. Practicing the technique as early as possible, as frequently as possible, provides the greatest benefit in the later stages of transition.

A person actively dying spends many hours seemingly

asleep or unconscious. We may hope our loved one is dreaming peacefully but worry he is suffering or being mentally tormented. When a person is practicing dying consciously, he has the tools to connect with his soul-mind or higher consciousness in deep meditation and continue to mentally process his life review while still in body. He will be able to use his visualization skills to continue practicing forgiveness, expressing gratitude, and purposefully releasing his physical attachments.

This is how taking the time to practice the technique for weeks or months prior to entering the active dying stage is beneficial, and why hospice volunteers and caregivers will be good transition guides simply because they have more time to spend with the dying. It is important for other health care workers to be aware so they can facilitate or participate in the process.

It is recommended that family transition guides practice and become comfortable with these exercises themselves before attempting to teach them to others. Use your own experience of it to help others learn to relax their bodies and minds, and participate consciously in their own visualization process.

If you are an experienced meditator, this exercise may seem quite elementary, but trust me, for most people it will be quite new and different. If you have been doing similar work previously, by all means continue with your preferred method. These are only suggestions.

Breathing exercises help keep the chest muscles flexible. They allow more oxygen to flow in with each breath and the lungs to empty completely on the exhalation. Breathing is done with less effort.

Surgical patients may be asked to do a similar breathing exercise before and after abdominal, heart, or lung surgery. This deep breathing can help prevent pneumonia when the patient is not able to get up and move around easily. It may help people with chronic obstructive pulmonary disease (COPD) and reduce symptoms caused by anxiety, fear and stress.

Anxiety, fear and stress increase the heart and breathing rates, and the body's demand for oxygen. Learning to control one's breathing rate also calms the brain's electrical activities and thought patterns. Breathing exercises help to keep the muscles and joints from stiffening, which can bring comfort and peace to the dying person.

Yoga postures with deep breathing keep the energy flowing throughout the body and the Chakras in alignment. A weekly yoga class can do wonders for achieving peace of mind and managing the caregiver's stress as well as the patient's.

Breath

This first technique involves learning to breathe correctly. Watch as an infant breathes, and notice that the abdomen rises and falls as she inhales and exhales. Tension turns us into shallow breathers.

Place one hand on your chest and the other on your abdomen at your diaphragm above your waistline, and breathe in normally and exhale. You may notice only the upper chest will rise and fall as you breathe in and out.

Next, inhale by allowing your abdomen to expand then exhale by contracting your abdomen, and notice the difference. The chest will rise and fall on its own.

Practice involves counting to establish a rhythmic pattern focusing on the breath — not on the breathing, not on the abdomen rising and falling, but on the energy that comes into the body as you breathe in, swirls around in your brain, circulates throughout your body, and leaves your body as you exhale.

As you focus on your breath, the rest of the world falls away and the body-mind becomes relaxed and peaceful. Practice breathing in and out, focusing on the breath often during the day, when going to sleep, before getting out of bed in the morning.

Physical Relaxation

The second technique involves relaxing the body. The Relaxation Exercises will alert you to places in your body where you hold tension or experience pain. By mentally directing the breath into those areas and focusing your attention on those areas, and noticing the tension melting away as you exhale, you are also directing your immune system to attend to those areas. Combining the tensing and relaxing the muscles exercise with breathing in and out, and focusing on the breath allows your muscles to relax and release the tension.

Mental Relaxation

When the person is relaxed and breathing rhythmically, introducing guided visualizations will help the person:

- Process his life review to let go of any matters that cause him concern
- Work on forgiveness and gratitude issues
- Count his blessings
- Experience letting go of his attachments to physical things and desires

- Visualize his ideas about heaven or life beyond physical life
- Remember all the love he expressed and received
- Visualize his journey out of his body and work on his Personal Transition Guidebook

Soul Connection

We have the ability to get in touch with our Higher Self, our Inner Wisdom. Once we awaken our connection to our soul, it will guide our life.

...the Kingdom of God is Within (Luke 17:20-21)

We can deepen our meditations by using rhythmic breathing and opening our heart (Chakra) center to our inner guidance to enhance our practice of conscious dying. It is here in the space between thoughts that we find God and experience unconditional love.

Breathing Exercise

Have the person sit or lie down, whatever is most comfortable. Ask the person to adjust his body so he doesn't feel any pressure or discomfort. Make sure the environment is quiet and safe, free from interruptions. Ask the person to begin by taking long slow deep breaths. Watch the person as he breathes — the abdomen should rise with the inhalation followed by the chest; the abdomen should fall before the chest with each exhalation. Reinforce this by speaking aloud:

Allow your abdomen to expand as you inhale, count to yourself (at your own speed) 1, 2, 3, 4, 5... hold for a few seconds counting 1, 2, 3 ... then slowly contract your abdomen as you exhale 1, 2, 3, 4, 5 ...

hold 2, 3 ... Breathe in 3, 4, 5 ... hold 2, 3 ... Exhale, 3, 4, 5 ... hold 2, 3 ...

Some people may find this difficult to do at first because they've forgotten how to breathe correctly. Most people will expand their chest only, not their abdomen, which doesn't fully use their lung capacity to send sufficient oxygen to the brain. This may help an actively dying person to maintain consciousness longer.

If the person has trouble coordinating the counting with the breathing, help him by doing the counting out loud. Your counting along with him allows him to focus on his breathing. Do it about ten times then just have him continue breathing without counting for a few minutes to experience the feeling of relaxation. When he is ready, count another ten breaths then relax.

Ask how he is feeling occasionally and address any concerns. Continue for about 20 minutes. Some people may experience a head rush and feel dizzy at first if their brain hasn't gotten that much oxygen lately — it'll pass.

After practicing this over several days, have the person do it without counting but maintaining the same rhythm. Suggest that he:

- Not be concerned about whether he does 10 or 6 or 15 breaths, just do what feels right
- Focus his attention on the breath — the energy coming in, the energy flowing out
- Imagine a feeling of warm water flowing over his body, filling every cell of his body, each time he inhales
- Imagine toxins and negativity oozing out through his fingertips and toes each time he exhales

Add the muscle relaxation exercise that follows once he has the breathing pattern down.

In this sample script, commas, periods and dots (...) are symbols for pauses, which may be adjusted according to the abilities of the person you are working with. Pause longer between paragraphs, shorter for commas. The words should be read slowly, but not monotone, in sync with the person's breathing.

Relaxation Exercise 1

Now that you are comfortable, begin to focus on your breath... as you inhale, notice that your abdomen rises ... as you exhale, notice that your abdomen falls ... breathe in deeply ... hold ... breathe out ... hold ... and again ... breathing in comfortably ... and hold ... exhale ah-h-h-h-h-h ... there is nothing you can do wrong ... whatever feels comfortable is right for you.

Continue to breathe ... in ... and out ... in ... and out ... feel the tension in your body begin to release as you continue to breathe ... in ... and out.

Now you're going to tense each small muscle group, one at a time, as you inhale, then relax each group as you exhale.

You'll notice that in tightening one group, another may also tense (for example, foot and calf), direct your attention to the oxygen flowing to only one muscle group at a time.

Focus your attention on the life-giving oxygen

flowing into each area as you tense, and the toxins and negativity flowing out as you relax. Notice the difference in your muscles, before and after each breath.

Let's begin by taking a few slow abdominal breaths ... You can use the count you found comfortable in the abdominal breathing exercise, including the hold in between breaths.

(PAUSE -1 minute)

Move your attention to your right foot ... inhale and tighten the muscles of your right foot ... hold ... exhale and relax the muscle ... and breathe ... again tense the muscles of your right foot ... hold ... and relax as you exhale ... and hold ... and breathe.

Now pay attention to your left foot, inhale as you tense ... and hold ... Exhale ... and hold ... and breathe ... Feel the tension in your left foot as you inhale ... and hold ... feel the letting go as you exhale ... and hold ... and breathe.

Move your attention to you right calf as you inhale ... hold ... exhale ... and breathe ... and again as you notice your abdomen rise as you tense the muscles of your right calf and hold ... Notice your abdomen fall as you exhale and the tension flows out of your calf muscles ... and breathe.

Now the left calf ... feel the tension as you inhale ... feel the relaxation as you exhale ... and breathe ... again with your left calf, tensing the muscles, feeling the tension, hold, and relax as you exhale and let go ... and breathe.

Move your attention to your right thigh ... tense those muscles ... hold ... relax those muscles ... and breathe ... again, tense those thigh muscles ... hold ... and relax as you exhale... and breathe.

Now your left thigh ... inhale and feel the tension ... exhale and feel the relaxation. Breathe in ... hold the tension in the thigh, and relax allowing the tension to flow out ... and breathe.

Turning your attention now to the lower part of your body, tense your pelvic area, abdomen and buttocks as you inhale, hold, and release as you relax and let go of the tension with your exhalation ... and breathe ... inhale and tense those muscles, hold, release the tension ... and breathe.

Moving your attention to your upper body, to your chest and back, tighten your upper body as you inhale and release the tension, feel the relaxation flow in as you exhale ... and breathe ... once again, tense those muscles, hold the tension, relax as you exhale ... and breathe.

Now pay attention to your right shoulder ... tense those muscles as you inhale, hold the tension, and relax as you exhale and feel the tension flow out ... and breathe ... again tense your right shoulder, Feel the tension as you hold, and release the tension as you exhale.

Now your left shoulder, inhale and feel the tension, hold it, exhale and let go of the tension ... and breathe ... inhale, tensing your left shoulder, hold, and relax as you exhale ... and breathe.

Now pay attention to your right upper arm ... tense those muscles as you inhale, hold the tension, and relax as you exhale and feel the tension flow out ... and breathe ... again tense your right upper arm, Feel the tension as you hold, and release the tension as you exhale.

Now your left upper arm, inhale and feel the tension, hold it, exhale and let go of the tension ... and breathe ... inhale, tensing your left upper arm, hold, and relax as you exhale ... and breathe.

Now your right forearm ... tense the muscles ... hold the tension ... relax the tension ... breathe ... and once again your right forearm ... tensing ... holding ... relaxing ... breathe.

Now your left forearm ... tense the muscles ... hold the tension ... relax the tension ... breathe ... and once again your left forearm ... tensing ... holding ... relaxing ... breathe.

Now your right hand ... tense the muscles ... hold the tension ... relax the tension ... breathe ... and once again your right hand ... tensing ... holding ... relaxing ... breathe.

Now your left hand ... tense the muscles ... hold the tension ... relax the tension ... breathe ... and once again your left hand ... tensing ... holding ... relaxing ... breathe.

Moving your attention now to you neck, tighten ... inhale ... relax ... breathe ... and again, tense the muscles ... hold it ... relax ... and breathe.

And now your head ... tense the muscles of your

face and scalp as you inhale, hold the tension, and relax as you exhale. Once again, crinkle up your face, hold it, and relax as you exhale and feel the tension flow out ... and breathe.

The areas where pain is experienced are where you hold your tension ... For most of us, it's in the neck and shoulders ... go back to those painful areas, and tense and relax those muscles several more times as you inhale and exhale.

You are getting in touch with your body, learning to read its signals, release the tension you hold in your muscles, and experience relaxation and peace.

Take a few minutes to tense and relax those areas that need more work remembering to allow your abdomen to rise with each inhalation and fall with each exhalation.

(PAUSE - 5 to 10 minutes)

It's time now to awaken from this relaxed state but you will remain relaxed even after you awaken. I'm going to count up from 1 to 5 ... with each number you will awaken a little more until I reach the number 5 and you will be fully awake and aware of your surroundings.

One ... you are beginning to come back to an awake state feeling relaxed and refreshed ... two ... you are awakening more, feeling happy and peaceful as if returning from a pleasant journey ... three ... you feel yourself becoming more and more aware of your surroundings, the chair you are sitting in, the room you are in ... four ... you continue to feel lighter and more relaxed every time you do this exercise ... five

... you are now fully awake and aware of where you are, feeling peaceful and relaxed, calm and happy.

Each person will progress at his own rate, but after doing the above exercise with him once a day for a week or when you feel he is ready, move on to the next script which calls attention to the large muscle groups: right leg, left leg, lower body, upper body, left arm, right arm, shoulders, neck and head. Do this for a couple of weeks until it feels quite natural to the person.

Relaxation Exercise 2

Now that you are comfortable, begin to focus on your breath ... as you inhale, notice that your abdomen rises... as you exhale, notice that your abdomen falls ... breathe in deeply ... hold ... breathe out ... hold ... and again... breathing in comfortably ... and hold ... exhale ah-h-h-h-h ... there is nothing you can do wrong ... whatever feels comfortable is right for you.

Continue to breathe ... in ... and out ... in ... and out ... feel the tension in your body begin to release as you continue to breathe ... in ... and out.

Now you're going to tense each large muscle group, one at a time, as you inhale, then relax each group as you exhale.

Direct your attention to the oxygen flowing in to only one muscle group at a time. Focus on the life-giving oxygen flowing into each area as you tense, and the toxins and negativity flowing out as you relax. Notice the difference in your muscles.

Let's begin by taking a few relaxing abdominal breaths.

(PAUSE - 1 minute)

Move your attention to your right leg ... inhale and tighten the muscles of your right leg ... hold ... exhale and relax the muscles ... and breathe ... again tense the muscles of your right leg ... hold ... and relax as you exhale ... and hold ... and breathe.

Now pay attention to your left leg, inhale as you tense ... and hold ... exhale ... and hold ... and breathe ...feel the tension in your left leg as you inhale ... and hold ... feel the letting go as you exhale ... and hold ... and breathe.

Turning your attention now to the lower part of your body, tense your pelvic area and buttocks as you inhale, hold, and release as you relax and let go of the tension with your exhalation ... and breathe ... inhale and tense those muscles again, hold, release the tension ... and breathe.

Moving your attention to your upper body, to your chest and back, tighten those muscles as you inhale and release the tension, feel the relaxation flow in as you exhale ... and breathe ... once again, tense those muscles, hold the tension, relax as you exhale ... and breathe.

Now pay attention to your right arm and hand ... tense those muscles as you inhale, hold the tension, and relax as you exhale and feel the tension flow out ... and breathe ... again tense your right arm, feel the tension as you hold, and release the tension as you exhale.

Now your left arm and hand, inhale and feel the tension, hold it, exhale and let go of the tension ... and breathe ... inhale, tensing your left arm, hold, and relax as you exhale ... and breathe.

Moving your attention now to your neck and head, tense the muscles of your face and scalp as you inhale, hold the tension, and relax as you exhale. Once again, crinkle up your face, tense your neck ... hold it, and relax as you exhale and feel the tension flow out ... and breathe.

You are becoming very relaxed, but you can relax even more by going back to any painful areas, and tense and relax those muscles several more times as you inhale and exhale. Take a few minutes to tense and relax those areas that need more work remembering to allow your abdomen to rise with each inhalation and fall with each exhalation.

(PAUSE - 5 to 10 minutes)

It's time now to awaken from this relaxed state but you will remain relaxed even after you awaken. I'm going to count up from 1 to 5 ... with each number you will awaken a little more until I reach the number 5 and you will be fully awake and aware of your surroundings.

One ... you are beginning to come back to an awake state feeling relaxed and refreshed ... two ... you are awakening more, feeling happy and peaceful as if returning from a pleasant journey ... three ... you feel yourself becoming more and more aware of your surroundings, the chair you are sitting in, the room you are in ... four ... you continue to feel lighter and more relaxed every time you do this exercise ... five ... you are now fully awake and aware of where you are, feeling peaceful and relaxed, calm and happy.

For practicing on your own, I have recorded Relaxation Exercise 1 and 2, which may be downloaded from my web site at BeyondtheVeil.net.

Once the person feels comfortable doing this exercise, is feeling peaceful and relaxed, suggest he continue on his own lying in bed as he is going to sleep or as often as he wants during the day. He may want to continue tensing and relaxing large or small muscle groups or he may want to scan his body for pain spots as in the following script.

Body Scan Exercise

As you continue finding your own rhythm for breathing in and breathing out, pay attention to your physical body starting at your feet ... breathing in ... and out slowly ... as you move your attention up your legs, notice any tension in the muscles in your feet ... breathing in ... and out ... as you move your attention up your legs, notice any tension in the muscles in your calves ... tighten and relax those muscles as you breathe ... your knees ... your thighs ... as you inhale, tense the muscles in each of those areas, one at a time ... relax them as you exhale ... and feel the tension flow away ... and the relaxation flow in as your muscles expand and relax like a rubber band.

(PAUSE for a few minutes to allow the person to do this based on his ability)

Continuing to breathe in and out ... move your attention up the trunk of your body ... the pelvic region, the buttocks, the abdomen, the chest, the back ... scan your body for pain or discomfort ... tense and relax the muscles ... direct the breath into that area ... do this as many times as necessary to release the tension and anxiety, and let go into a state of peace and relaxation as you continue to focus on your breathing in and breathing out.

(PAUSE for a few minutes to allow the person to do this based on his ability)

Continuing to breathe ... turn your attention now to your upper body ... your neck, your head, your face ... tense the muscles of your brow as you inhale ... relax them as you exhale ... tense the muscles of your whole face ... your neck ... your scalp ... relax those muscles ... let go of the tension ... let go of your fears ... release your anxiety ... just breathe into it and let it go.

(PAUSE for a few minutes to allow the person to do this based on her ability)

Continue breathing in and out slowly as you scan your physical form once more from your toes to your head and stop to release any tension that remains.

(PAUSE for a few minutes to allow the person to do this based on his ability)

When you feel the person has mastered the muscle relaxation technique, she can practice doing the abdominal breathing while tensing and relaxing her entire body or isolate large or small muscle groups as needed. It will be different for different people. Having a selection of peaceful meditation music like *Healing* by ShapeshifterDNA (see *Bibliography*) around is helpful for guided visualizations or one's own inner explorations.

Notice that the time required to do these exercises has lessened considerably from isolating small muscle groups to whole body relaxation. Have the person use the rest of the 20-30 minutes to practice using a focus technique (below). This may help him achieve a deeper state of relaxation more quickly.

After several months of practice, anyone should be able to use this exercise, tensing and relaxing the whole body by taking one or two deep breaths, while stopped in their car in rush hour traffic, standing in line at the grocery store, or just before they go to sleep at night to shift quickly into a peaceful state of calmness and relaxation. An actively dying person can use it every time she closes her eyes.

Focus Techniques

Focus techniques help quiet the mental chatter. Some people have no problem shutting off the voices or images in their heads and focusing on one thought; others insist they can't get their thoughts to stop. Suggest to someone who has trouble stopping the constant chatter or the picture images flowing through his mind to allow them to rise and fall like ocean waves without paying attention to them as he continues practicing these techniques several times a day (practice, practice, practice).

Choose the technique that is most appealing to you and practice it consistently. Eventually, the conscious mind becomes frustrated (it wants to think, think, think) and allows the person to move into a superconscious state where there is no thought. The conscious mind can only focus on one thought at a time, the person gets to make the choice about which thought — or no thought, gets priority. Once you recognize the place of no-thought, it will be easier to get back to it and hold it from then on.

Counting

Imagine you are moving down an escalator as you count slowly down from 10 to 1, going down deeper with each number. Or count backwards from 100 by 7s to give your left-brain something to think about while your right brain imagines you are floating on a fluffy white cloud.

Sound/Chant

Choose a word like Peace, Love, Relax or simply the word One, or a word related to your religious beliefs, such as God, Jesus, Allah, Buddha, or a mantra like *Om Mani Padme Hum.* Each time you exhale, say the word out loud or to yourself, drawing the sound out the length of the exhalation.

The sounds of Ah and Om give off good vibrations, especially when vocalized as you exhale, but may also be said to yourself. When vocalized, Om sounds like Aum, drawn out the length of the breath, *Au-u-um-m-m-m-m.* Ah is the natural sound of exhaling, *ah-h-h-h-h-h-h...*

Candle

Light a candle in front of where you are sitting. Close your eyes and do several minutes of deep breathing. When you feel very relaxed, open your eyes and stare at the flame as long as you can with your eyes open (avoid crossing your eyes).

When you close your eyes, an after image of the flame will appear in the darkness. It will become smaller and smaller, seeming to recede in the distance, but hold the image as long as you can. Watch as it transforms into a beautiful, shimmering Blue Jewel (which is likely to take a good deal of practice).

Full Moon
This gives the same effect as the candle flame for the outdoorsy types. And, for both the candle and the full moon, when the image fades, open your eyes and stare at it again until you have to close your eyes, and again hold the image as long as you can.

Mandalas
These are usually circular drawings with detailed geometric line art inside the circle and a central focal point, often colorful and intricate. Stare at the center of a mandala as long as you can. Close your eyes and experience the after-image. Calmly explore whatever happens for you visually.

Visualizing the Chakra System

The purpose of the heart is to know your self,
to be your self, and yet one with God.
~ Edgar Cayce

For this exercise, you'll be using your imagination to visualize a field of energy surrounding and interpenetrating your physical body at seven points along your spinal column from the base of your spine to the top of your head.

Each energy center or Chakra may be visualized as a dynamic vortex of colored light surrounding a downturned bowl, which you will be turning over to catch the light that runs from Source down your spinal column and back up, crisscrossing at these energy centers and activating the glands of the sympathetic nervous system.

Each center is associated with your emotions and your sense of self, and relates to balance in your life. If a center is blocked (e.g., by an emotion you have been holding onto like anger or jealousy), you will train yourself to clear it and return to balance.

When the energy flows freely within the balanced system, the person may experience a clarity of mind or, as Eastern religions suggest, an opening of the Third Eye and a heightened awareness of being connected to the Source.

Doing this exercise on a regular basis can help you maintain a peaceful state of mind and a balanced state of health by releasing toxins and traumas (negative energy) from the body-mind. It is also a good exercise to use before doing forgiveness or gratitude work as it puts you in a loving space where some of these difficult issues are easier to work through or reconcile. Adding some music like the *Odyssey Chakra Balancing* soundscape by ShapeshifterDNA (see *Bibliography*) will help you to flow more easily with this process.

Following is a basic description of this energy system and associated glands so you can begin to connect your emotions with the affected Chakra:

1st Root Chakra: prostrate/ovaries
- Color: Red
- Passion, vitality, desire, energy
- Imbalance = rigid beliefs, hate, anger, pettiness, jealousy, prejudice
- Balance = flexible, adaptable, accepting, able to flow with changes

2nd Sacral Chakra: coccyx/spleen
- Color: Orange
- Joy, sociability, center of intimacy and well-being, controls our appetites (food, sex, pleasure)
- Imbalance = lack of control, addictions, blames others
- Balance = internal locus of control, ability to let go

3rd Solar Plexus Chakra: navel area/liver
- Color: Yellow
- Intelligence, clarity, happiness, creativity, your personal power, intuition
- Imbalance = worthlessness, discouragement, uncertainty, need to control others
- Balance = become aware of worth, esteem and true power

4th Heart Chakra: thymus gland
- Color: Green
- Healing, harmony, nurturing
- Imbalance = inability to give and receive love, codependency, dysfunctional relationships, depression
- Balance = accept people as they are and love them anyway

5th Throat Chakra: thyroid gland
- Color: Blue
- Friendship, loyalty, open & honest communication
- Imbalance = shut down from grief or unexpressed feelings like anger and fear; abuse, dishonesty, drug use
- Balance = speak your truth, gateway to higher spiritual realms

6th Third Eye Chakra: pituitary gland
- Color: Indigo
- Meditation, Higher Self, self-awareness; ethical and philosophical principles
- Imbalance = narrow minded, self-righteous, fundamentalist
- Balance = opens the mind to truth; gives us wisdom, discernment, imagination and knowledge

7th Crown Chakra: pineal gland
- Color: Violet
- Spiritual attainment, silent contemplation,

eternal truth, higher purpose, enlightenment

- Imbalance = self-centered, egotistical, delusions of grandeur
- Balance = Self-Realization, connection to the Divine, contemplative, brings healing and transformation

This exercise may be done sitting cross-legged in lotus posture or in a straight-back chair with feet flat on the floor, hands resting on knees, thumb and index finger touching with other three fingers straight or the back of one hand resting on the palm of the other on the lap. If the person is bed-ridden, lying on the back with arms at the side will be fine.

Clearing the Chakras

Begin by doing a few minutes of deep breathing and muscle relaxation, and then:

Visualize a warm light, like a blanket, drifting down from above, surrounding your body with love and feelings of peace from head to toe.

(PAUSE)

The next time you exhale, let out a low sigh or a sound like ah-h-h-h-h-h or au- u-u-m-m-m-m and follow the sound vibration down, down, down, into a deep, pleasant, relaxed state of consciousness.

As you continue focusing on the inflow and outflow of your breath, shift away from your thoughts and emotions toward a state of inner peace and tranquility.

As you move into this higher state of mind you are beginning to experience your True Self as a powerful form of energy surrounding and interpenetrating your physical body. Allow yourself to visualize that in any way that feels right to you.

(PAUSE)

Step out of your body for a moment and notice that a beam of white light enters your Crown Chakra from above. It travels down the center of your physical spine, down your legs through your feet and into the earth ... it loops back through your body and returns to Source ... see and feel this energy as it moves through you in a continuous loop.

Focus your attention on the area around the base of your spine. See this energy become a radiating, swirling ball of red light. As you breathe in and out, see it spinning faster, the red light becoming brighter.

If you notice any dark spots, ask the white light to clear them for you.

If you feel any congestion around feelings of anger or rigid beliefs, ask the white light to cleanse them from your consciousness and allow you to move on peacefully with the flow of change in your life. Surround them with a pink bubble and allow them to drift away.

Imagine now the bowl at the base of your spine turning over, expanding and opening to catch the white light pouring into it, cleansing and balancing the energy.

Continue to breathe into this chakra until you feel the blockage has been removed and see the red ball of energy spinning smoothly.

(PAUSE)

Next focus your attention on the area of your body around your navel. See this energy as a radiating, swirling ball of orange light. As you breathe in and out, see it spinning faster, the orange light becoming brighter.

If you notice any dark spots, ask the white light to clear them for you.

If you feel any congestion or blockages concerning addictions to the physical world whether it is to food, things or people ... just allow them to be, without clinging to them, and let them go. Surround them with a pink bubble and allow them drift away.

Imagine now the bowl at your navel turning over, expanding and opening to catch the white light pouring into it, cleansing and balancing the energy.

Continue to breathe into this chakra until you feel the blockage has been removed and see the orange ball of energy spinning smoothly.

(PAUSE)

Next focus your attention on the area of your body around your solar plexus. See this energy as a radiating, swirling ball of yellow light. As you breathe in and out, see it spinning faster, the yellow light becoming brighter.

If you notice any dark spots, ask the white light to clear them for you.

If you feel any congestion or blockages concerning your self-worth or your sense of self ... surround them with a pink bubble and allow them to drift away. Become aware of your true power as a spiritual being with meaning and purpose in your life.

Imagine now the bowl at your solar plexus turning over, expanding and opening to catch the white light pouring into it, cleansing and balancing the energy.

Continue to breathe into this chakra until you feel the blockage has been removed and see the yellow ball of energy spinning smoothly.

(PAUSE)

Next focus your attention on the area of your body around your heart. See this energy as a radiating, swirling ball of green light. As you breathe in and out, see it spinning faster, the green light becoming brighter.

If you notice any dark spots, ask the white light to clear them for you.

If you feel any congestion or blockages concerning your ability to give and receive love ... surround them with a pink bubble and allow them to drift away. See yourself accepting people as they are with all their flaws and love them anyway. Allow the love in your heart to expand to include all sentient beings.

Imagine now the bowl at your heart center turning over, expanding and opening to catch the white light pouring into it, cleansing and balancing the energy.

Continue to breathe into this chakra until you feel the blockage has been removed and see the green ball of energy spinning smoothly.

(PAUSE)

Next focus your attention on the area of your body around your neck and throat. See this energy as a radiating, swirling ball of blue light. As you breathe in and out, see it spinning faster, the blue light becoming brighter.

If you notice any dark spots, ask the white light to clear them for you.

If you have shut yourself down over grief or unexpressed negative feelings about your life or people around you, now is the time to let them go on to find their highest good. Surround them with a pink bubble and allow them to drift away. Open this gateway to higher spiritual realms where you can find your real voice and speak your truth.

Imagine now the bowl at your throat turning over, expanding and opening to catch the white light pouring into it, cleansing and balancing the energy.

Continue to breathe into this chakra until you feel the blockage has been removed and see the blue ball of energy spinning smoothly.

(PAUSE)

Next focus your attention on the area of your body around your forehead between your eyes, on your Third Eye. See this energy as a radiating, swirling ball of indigo blue light. As you breathe in and out, see it spinning faster, the blue light becoming brighter.

If you notice any dark spots, ask the white light to clear them for you.

If you feel any congestion or blockages because you have been narrow-minded, judgmental or self-righteous in your beliefs or the way you treat other people... surround them with a pink bubble and allow them to drift away. Open your mind to the greater wisdom that lies within and see the truth as it is revealed to you.

Imagine now the bowl at your third eye turning over, expanding and opening to catch the white light pouring into it, cleansing and balancing the energy.

Continue to breathe into this chakra until you feel the blockage has been removed and see the blue ball of energy spinning smoothly.

(PAUSE)

Next focus your attention on the area of your body around the top of your head. See this energy as a radiating, swirling ball of violet light. As you breathe in and out, see it spinning faster, the violet light becoming brighter.

If you notice any dark spots, ask the white light to clear them for you.

If you have any congestion or blockages that leave you feeling spiritually disconnected or empty or strongly attached to your body and the physical world ... surround them with a pink bubble and allow them to drift away. Become aware of your true power as a spiritual being with meaning and purpose in your life.

Imagine now the bowl at your top of your head turning over, expanding and opening to catch the white light pouring into it, cleansing and balancing the energy.

Continue to breathe into this chakra until you feel the blockage has been removed and see the violet ball of energy spinning smoothly, allowing the white light to pass freely into your crown chakra, through all your chakras and out again, surrounding your body with this all loving energy.

Notice the energy of your light flowing smoothly from the top of your head to your root chakra, down your legs into the earth and back again, surrounding your body with peace and joy... the light is continuously cleansing and purifying your energy... you are feeling lighter and lighter... filled with Divine love and light.

You are feeling peaceful and relaxed ... in harmony with your body-mind-spirit... at one with the Source of your being. Continue breathing and relaxing for as long as you want.

NOTES · NOTES · NOTES · NOTES · NOTES

Chapter 4

"I discovered the secret of the sea in meditation upon a dewdrop."
~ Kahlil Gibran

Script Writing for Guided Visualizations

Several years after my NDE, I took a class in self-hypnosis to help me deal with the post-traumatic stress caused by that enigmatic experience. This led me into meditation, yoga, psychosynthesis, metaphysics, parapsychology, eastern religions and ancient wisdom teachings, which accelerated my spiritual development.

Ten years after I graduated from the university, I pursued a second master's degree in clinical hypnotherapy, which helped me learn how to talk to the subconscious mind using the techniques of guided visualization. For many years in the early 1990s, I specialized in past life regression as a therapy for people dealing with deeply repressed emotions that couldn't be resolved through traditional therapies or age regression.

Around the same time, I became an ordained minister and a spiritual counselor helping people to get in touch with their inner wisdom. It was through this work that I developed this method of teaching the Art of Conscious Dying and eventually created a training program to teach paraprofessionals how to incorporate the Art of Conscious Dying into their work. I realized I needed to create a demand for their services as Transition Guides and so I released a short, introductory version called *Beginner's Guide to Conscious Dying*.

After that book had been out for a while, I realized I didn't want to be traveling around the country doing training sessions while spending half my life in airports and hotels, so I created this more complete version to make it available to anyone who is interested in learning this practice of conscious dying. I decided to include this chapter, which was not in the first ebook edition, on script writing for caregivers who want to learn to work with their patients in this area. If you are reading this book for yourself, you might want to enlist a caregiver to read your personal guidebook or make your own recordings.

As a transition guide, there are some things you'll need to pay attention to as far as wording if you are going to write your own guided visualization scripts. It is better to write out the words and rehearse them so negative words or ideas don't accidentally slip out off the top of your head. Avoid using words like *no, never, not, none, nothing, can't, don't, won't* as the subconscious mind ignores negative words. There are exceptions when appropriate to make a statement positive (e.g., *Don't listen to what I'm saying* is decoded as Listen to what I'm saying).

The way suggestions are worded and how you say them are very important. Depending on where you put the emphasis, the meaning may change. Underline words you want to emphasize to be sure the meaning is clear. Read aloud what you've written before you finalize your script to listen to the rhythm.

Working with the Subconscious Mind

The subconscious mind doesn't know the difference between a metaphor and a real story. It accepts everything literally and a person will take action in the way her mind has interpreted the suggestion according to her underlying belief system.

Making positive suggestions; using I am, I can, I will statements and putting emphasis on the correct words; using words and statements about peace, love, hope, courage, kindness, compassion, trust, comfort, helps the conscious mind relax while the subconscious remains open to further positive suggestions.

For the power of suggestion to be effective, there must be a clear and definite message with no ambiguity. You're not trying to program somebody yet there must be clear goals and a series of suggestions related to achieving that goal. Suggestions must be repeated in different ways to reinforce the same idea, don't just repeat the same phrase over and over.

You are growing stronger every day. Each day you feel yourself becoming stronger and healthier. Every time you inhale, you feel strength and vitality spreading throughout your body. During the coming week, your strength will improve more and more each day.

When a scene is described, the person develops a mental image of the goal and the suggestion becomes even more effective. The subconscious mind receives the image as if it were real and the person acts on that belief. That's why guided visualizations that include a story are particularly powerful.

The subconscious mind is the storehouse of memories and the emotions attached to them. Some of these memories are repressed as a protective mechanism in childhood and act as blockages in our energy system. They may have been comforting and protective when we were children but may be holding us back as adults.

It is not necessary to bring them into conscious awareness; however, the energy can be dissipated using imagery (surrounding them in a pink bubble and floating them away) or ritual (writing about them and burning the paper).

When doing a guided visualization to help a person release negative patterns during forgiveness work, such as during a life review exercise, you will be working with the subconscious mind and the emotions. Determine the person's intentions before writing the script (e.g., work on forgiveness, express gratitude, resolve issues with a loved one, let go of anger). Whatever the issue is, it may be further referred to as "that problem." The subconscious knows exactly what that problem is and which past events are involved.

After you have relaxed the person using a brief breathing and relaxation induction, begin by telling a story or describing a journey such as:

You are walking across a beautiful meadow (describe blue sky, clouds, birds, flowers, deer, rabbits, etc. to make it seem more realistic and compelling).

You see a peaceful, calm blue lake surrounded by (aspens, weeping willows, tall pines, snow-capped mountain peaks in the distance).

You feel the warmth of the sun on your skin.

You smell the (flowers or the pine trees or the sea).

Suggest as the person approaches the water's edge, she notices a boat tied to a tree with a rope. Tell her to walk toward it, untie the rope and step onto the boat, sit down and relax as it slowly and silently glides across the clear, calm water where she can see clearly, deep down into the water. The lake is a metaphor for the subconscious mind. Water relates to the emotions.

After cruising around for a while enjoying the warmth of the sun and a gentle breeze on her skin, suggest she go inside the cabin of the boat and close the watertight door. Suggest that she notices the boat has become a submarine and is sliding slowly *down, down, down* under the water as she watches out the portholes and sees a variety of colorful fish swimming past her eyes.

Describe the environment briefly then allow the person time to silently explore her own inner world. As the boat goes deeper and deeper below the surface, have her concentrate on the images she sees through the portholes appearing and disappearing, coming in and out of focus.

Have the person silently declare her intention then tell her to just observe what comes up from the depths without analyzing, criticizing, or judging, and to thank and bless each one for helping her on her life's journey. Give the person some silent time to process this imagery until you intuitively sense it is time to bring her back to the surface.

You can suggest that the person doesn't have to consciously remember any of this experience, that the subconscious mind will continue to work on the problem as long as it needs to until it is resolved and dissolved, and, as soon as it is, she will feel a great weight lifted off of her. Some people may report that they fell asleep and don't remember any of it, but days, weeks later, may report feeling lighter for some unknown reason.

Some problems may be resolved in one session; other problems go deeper and may take many sessions. Our soul knows all about us and is always ready to help when we ask — although not necessarily in the way or time frame we expect. This work may help bring peace of mind to a human being who is troubled by past events or has held onto family or personal secrets far too long.

If, in earlier discussions, the person tells you she wants to remember some troubling incident, you can suggest to her that she will remember whatever information will be helpful to her to resolve the issue and dissolve the karma. Mention also that she will be able to look at the information dispassionately and objectively so she can understand the lesson it came into her life to teach her. It provides a different perspective that often evokes "Aha!" moments.

If a person seems to be reliving a bad memory, remind her to return to her deep breathing feeling calm and relaxed. Remind her to just be the observer; that this was in the past and no longer has any power over her. Suggest it can help her understand why she is so angry, sad, fearful, and that she will be able to let go of that energy and be free of the affect it had on her during this life. Give the person's subconscious mind time to process the issue before counting her back up.

If, at any time, you get a sense that the person needs to come back to conscious awareness immediately, say, in normal tone of voice:

I'm going to count you up from 1 to 5 and with each number your breathing will return to normal and you will return to full consciousness, feeling more calm and relaxed.

Then quickly... *1, 2, 3, 4, 5.*

Remind her to take slow, deep breaths and return to her peaceful state of relaxation.

If the person encountered a difficult issue, which caused her to become restless or irritated after counting her up, get her to talk about what happened and see the issue from a new perspective. Help calm her breathing before talking if it seems necessary.

Another technique to use if a person seems distressed is to suggest she move on to a higher level of awareness or move ahead 5 years and describe the outcome, or to become the observer and watch the scene from above or see it from another perspective, while reminding her to focus on the breath and the feelings of relaxation.

When you sense the time is right (usually after 15 to 30 minutes), continue the guided journey of the boat slowly returning to the surface, rising toward the sunlight, slowly counting up from 1 to 5 with messages of feeling calm and relaxed, free from the pain of the past and feeling filled with hope and peace and love — gliding across the smooth lake, landing gently on the shore where she gets out of the boat and ties the rope to the tree.

With her new found freedom (from that problem), have her dancing in the sunlight, lying in the meadow looking up at the clouds and blue sky, feeling light and free. Allow her to enjoy this quiet, peaceful feeling for 10-15 minutes.

If a person is a habitual negative thinker, filled with anxiety, depressed, angry, ungrateful, hateful, you're going to have trouble convincing her positive thinking works. Some people actually want to hold onto their undesirable thoughts, may even find it amusing to get angry at others or about everything. You can talk about it in terms of how negative emotions affect their health and ask them to make a decision to let go of some of their physical symptoms/pain/discomfort.

Write a guided visualization script that describes a journey from a dark place to a light place, from a sad place to a happy place (from a subterranean cave out to sun bathed cliffs by the sea, from a dense forest to an aspen lined river and a golden meadow, from the bottom of a mountain to the top), to open her to a new perspective on life.

Even if she is actively dying, the person can envision a peaceful place inside and reach acceptance of the death of her body and the liberation of her soul. It takes the mind off any pain and suffering, and keeps it centered on the beauty of nature, the prospect of a joy filled life after death, and seeing loved ones again.

Using Indirect Suggestions

With indirect suggestions, the person doesn't have to verbalize or analyze a problem, doesn't even have to be consciously aware of the causes, which allows the subconscious mind to work out the solutions. Indirect suggestions set the sub-conscious into action to find records of past memories related to the suggestion and cause an automatic response.

When suggestions are given indirectly, the subconscious sorts it out and reorganizes the thoughts without the limitations, criticisms and judgments of the conscious mind. Suggest that the subconscious mind will dissolve the karma and resolve the issue without help from the conscious mind so the person will be free to be present with her dying process, with her family, with each precious last moment.

People will react to words according to their own understanding — don't assume others know what you mean. Meaning is in the mind of the person receiving the information and depends on context and connotation. Language influences peoples' perceptions, attitudes, feelings, and behaviors.

Indirect suggestions produce effects according to previous knowledge and experience that may not be known consciously. Words have different definitions in different areas of the country/world and definitions change over time. Unless you know the person well, stick to common expressions and word usage.

Automatic Responses

The following kinds of statements may be inserted into guided visualization scripts. Some relate to healing, others to forgiveness work.

For a person who is anxious and fearful, who probably has hypertension, this script will let her know how she can automatically respond to the suggestion to relax and let go.

You automatically know how to experience the pleasant sensation of a cool breeze on a warm, summer day.

Allow yourself to experience that sensation now.

(PAUSE for 30 seconds)

You automatically know how to become peaceful and relaxed by returning to your rhythmic breathing pattern.

Allow yourself to experience that sensation now.

(PAUSE for 30 seconds)

You automatically know how to lower your blood pressure, calm your nerves and become completely relaxed and peaceful.

Allow yourself to experience that sensation now.

(PAUSE for 30 seconds)

People generally don't want to feel they are being controlled or manipulated. Give them the freedom to make choices.

You may want to close your eyes or you may want to leave them open. Your eyes will close automatically when you are comfortable and relaxed.

As you continue to breathe easily and freely, you may notice that your eyelids are becoming so relaxed that you prefer that they remain closed until I tell you to open your eyes.

This could be for resisting, skeptical people or for those working on resolving past traumatic events or relationships. All issues don't have to come into conscious awareness to be resolved; some may be resolved on deeper levels.

You may be going through an emotionally corrective experience right now, without being consciously aware of the details ... just allow it to continue as you return your attention to your breathing ... you can be surprised and happy to notice how much lighter you feel when you awaken.

If abuse or molestation is a possibility, if guilt or shame is involved, the memories may be so painful a person may not have been able to confront them on a conscious level. Once the information is released by the subconscious mind, the person may finally be able to give a voice to her pain and release that negative energy from her body.

Secret memories you have never told anyone can be reviewed calmly by your subconscious mind to work out a solution to that problem.

You are permitting your subconscious mind to process the information in a way that is for your highest good ... you will awaken with a sense of relief and freedom knowing that problem has been resolved and dissolved.

This may reassure a person who might doze off or feel anxious about doing it right. Notice the use of the word *don't* which the subconscious mind will ignore making it a positive statement.

You don't have to listen to the words I'm saying... your subconscious mind will hear every word I say and will cause you to respond in just the right way.

Your subconscious mind will automatically do just what it needs to do in order to resolve that problem for good.

Give people more than one alternative putting the most difficult first.

Your subconscious mind will resolve that problem while I am here or after I leave.

Other Suggestions
Stay away from using big words, technical words, vague words, ethnic phrases, sayings or metaphors that may easily be misunderstood or misinterpreted by different cultures, but storytelling is a good way to distract the conscious mind so the subconscious can work out the problem without interference.

Occasionally observe the person's facial expressions, breathing, postures, and body movements during script reading and make adjustments (read faster or slower, pause longer or go on) by the reactions you notice.

If a person starts snoring or has obviously gone to sleep, pause for a minute then speak in your normal tone and say something like:

It may seem that you have gone to sleep but your subconscious mind is continuing to work on that problem ... your subconscious mind continues to listen to the sound of my voice, all you need to do is pay attention to your breathing.

Then go on reading your script. This slightly jars the person almost back to consciousness, immediately reassures her that all is well, and reminds her where to focus her attention.

The same happens after a long pause before you state you are going to count the person back up from 1 to 5. Begin speaking in a normal tone, which will slowly bring the person back to awareness of her surroundings but doesn't fully awaken her until you get to 5. After each number, say she is awakening a little more with each number.

As it turns out, the deepest state a person reaches is often during those last few minutes as you are counting from 1 to 5. Some people may prefer to be left alone in peace following these sessions; others may want to talk about their inner experiences before they forget. As you work with people over time, you will become familiar with their preferences.

Guided Life Reviews

Many near-death experiencers have reported seeing their lives pass before their eyes. Some describe this life review as a slideshow or a movie; others, as being immersed in the experience as if they are in it, feeling everything they felt and the feelings of others who were affected by their actions or words, for good and for bad.

NDErs have described being shown how magnificent even the smallest expressions of kindness and compassion they expressed toward others affected other people they never knew. They were shown the darkness they spread with their thoughts of anger, hatred, greed, or revenge toward other human beings.

The only important questions are, *did you learn what you went to earth to learn and did you express unconditional love while you were there?* Those who did not, get to re-live those lessons from their previous life which they failed to learn. This is karmic energy in action. The mental images are one's own thoughts.

Some of these lessons we will decide to bring into our next incarnation as we continue learning to be more forgiving, more compassionate, and more caring in personal relationships and of all life on the planet. This is the evolution of consciousness in action... the path of individual soul growth and development.

Reports from NDErs who described "hellish" experiences said they were faced with frightening images that arose out of the darkness in threatening ways. These are their own thought-forms arising from the depths of their subconscious, not a *place* of torment (like *hell*).

It could be their vision of what they thought they deserved for having the angry, violent thoughts they acted on before their bodies died. It could be the religious beliefs they held about hell and punishment for being an evil person.

In any case, it seems not being a compassionate and forgiving person in life can apparently manifest in some rather nasty special effects on the other side until one turns to the Light or rebirth becomes inevitable, or as the *Tibetan Book of the Dead* describes it, a harrowing 49-day journey through the Bardo searching for a suitable body to reincarnate once again. However, rather than rebirth being a punishment, it is another amazing opportunity to study at the University of Life on Earth where one hopes to remember who we really are and why we become human in that lifetime.

A question many people have asked me over the years concerns those who are especially cruel or vicious towards others, usually referring to people like Hitler, Pol Pot, Idi Amin, Saddam Hussein, Gaddafi, and serial killers, child molesters, slave traders, rapists, etc. It seems we would all want them sent to Hell if such a place existed. But there is no such place, any more than Heaven is a place, much as we would like to think so.

No question their life reviews were a purifying experience for their souls, which quickly reincarnated to deal with the negative karma they accumulated. In many subsequent incarnations, they may well experience lifetimes as victims in equal measure.

I've heard it said that if we didn't have people like these to show us what evil is we wouldn't understand compassion, much less unconditional love. And what about their victims, what might their transition experience be like? Was this their pre-birth plan in which they agreed to experience this extreme victimization together in this lifetime? Did their sacrifice advance them to greater frequencies of light and are they beginning to reincarnate to bring a higher consciousness perspective to humanity?

It is beyond the scope of this book to get further into this discussion except to say that if we were a murderer in one life, we may be the victim in another, the spouse or the child or parent of a murderer or a victim in other lifetimes, as becoming human is to learn about expressing compassion through different relationships as we learn to manifest unconditional love in the physical world and learn to live in peace and harmony with each other and the planet.

We have all been each other in one lifetime or another. We are learning these lessons here for the benefit of our soul's growth beyond the veil. We are not just human beings; we are spiritual/human beings.

As *thoughts are things,* one must be careful where her thoughts dwell. People who harbor dark and ugly thoughts may want to consider releasing them from their minds by learning to express gratitude and forgiveness before their body dies so they don't meet those dark and uglies during their life review. You think no one knows your inner thoughts, but your soul knows. There is nowhere to hide.

When we compare NDE descriptions and related religious beliefs of people around the world, it's reasonable to conclude that people get what they expect — at least at first. If one believes he will see Jesus or streets paved with gold or hellfire and brimstone, that's apparently what he'll see. If you believe you will be punished, it will seem as if you are. If you believe dead is dead and life ends at death, that's how it will seem to you at first — but then your consciousness will expand and you will see something quite extraordinary!

We can use positive visualizations to practice dying before our bodies die to ease us into transition when our time comes and make it a peaceful, joyous journey back home to Source. This is similar to the purpose of the Egyptian and Tibetan Books of the Dead, couched in modern day terms.

We can write our own *book of the dead* based on our own beliefs to reconcile our life before our body dies and hopefully take us on a journey into higher consciousness as we cross the threshold from this life to the next by writing it into one's Personal Transition Guidebook.

Once the person you're working with has the breathing and muscle relaxation techniques down, you can introduce guided visualization to help him engage his imagination and creativity to design a peaceful place in his mind to do his inner work (life review, forgiveness and gratitude healing, letting go of attachments). Long before it becomes necessary, anyone can practice these techniques, perhaps as part of a once a month cleansing or purifying ritual.

People undergoing medical treatments, like chemo-therapy or dialysis, can wear headphones and listen to relaxing music and guided visualizations to relax themselves further while undergoing the procedures or before surgeries.

Those dying often have little to do but sit in a chair or

lie in bed and think. What goes through their minds are often fear-filled thoughts about what's going to happen to them when their body dies. Giving them peaceful guided visualizations and relaxing music to listen to may help relieve their anxiety and allow them to do the inner work they need to do.

Religions provide people with prayers to memorize to fill their minds and many people close to death continually say their Rosary or recite Bible verses or other religious text. Some people don't know what to think about or even how to think depending on the lives they've lived and the beliefs they've formed about death, dying and any possible afterlife.

There are those who find comfort in their religion or traditions for answers; others are sure life has no meaning beyond accumulating the most toys or having the most money and power. Then there are those who know there is more to life than this life and this planet, and actually look forward to returning home to their soul family on the other side.

Some people are able to visualize easily, others may have trouble at first. Some need more techniques and practice with a coach who can work with them one-on-one over a period of time. A transition guide may need to start with simpler imagery to get a person comfortable with visualizing.

First, to determine if a person is able to visualize at all, ask her to close her eyes and imagine she is standing in front of her house, walking up to the front door. Then ask her to visualize the door, where the doorknob or handle is, where the lock is, whether there is a screen door or storm door, what the door is made of, what color it is, where the doorbell is. Ask her to imagine her hand reaching for the handle, opening the door, walking inside the house, looking around — ask *what do you see?*

Some people can visualize it clearly, some sense it in other ways, and some may say they see only blackness. By how they describe what they see or don't see, you'll know how to write their guided visualization scripts. If they see nothing, simply ask them to imagine they do for the time being. They will eventually catch on.

Close the doors and windows so there is as little noise as possible. Turn off the cell phones. Put a "do not disturb" sign on the door. Put a cover over the birdcage. Close the curtains; turn down the lights. If the person likes, peaceful meditation or environmental music may be played softly in the background. An excellent piece of music for this is *Healing* by ShapeshifterDNA. The person may close her eyes or leave them open (they will close on their own). After you sense she is comfortable, begin reading the script following her breathing pattern.

Creating Your Inner Workspace

Notice now that as you breathe in, your abdomen rises ... as you breathe out, your abdomen falls ... in ... and out ... in ... and out ... expand your abdomen as you inhale ... contract your abdomen as you exhale ... tense all the muscles in your body as you breathe in ... relax all the muscles in your body as you breathe out ... again breathe in ... and relax ... tense ... exhale ... inhale ... relax.

(PAUSE for a minute or two)

Continue to breathe ... and relax ... inhale ... let go ... breathe ... and relax ... feel the tension in your body falling away as you relax more and more ... feel the confusion in your mind giving way to peace, and only pay attention to the energy coming in ... the energy flowing out ... allow your thoughts to drift through your mind [like leaves falling from the trees or balloons drifting with the wind or birds in silent flight] without paying attention to them as you return your awareness to your breathing in and breathing out ... breathing in ... breathing out ... breathing in ... breathing out ... relaxing ... letting go.

(PAUSE for a minute or two)

You feel yourself drifting up out of your body ... above the bed ... away from this room ... away from this building ... floating on a fluffy white cloud surrounded by a blue sky ... you may hear birds singing ... water flowing gently downstream ... soft music playing off in the distance ... you are feeling very relaxed and comfortable ... it is peaceful all around you ... your breathing has become rhythmic and your body is relaxed ... your mind is at peace.

(PAUSE for a minute or two)

Somewhere in your memory there is a place of complete peace and relaxation ... you feel yourself being drawn back to that place now ... imagine a shape and make that the shape of this place ... imagine a color and make that the color of this place ... it could be indoors or outdoors ... it could be on this planet or another ... it could be familiar or completely different from any place you've seen before ... when you have this place in your mind, I want you to enter into it ... walk around in it ... get a feel for it ... try it on for size ... if you don't like it after all, find another or change it any way you like.

(PAUSE for a minute or two)

When you are sure this is your special place, decorate it any way you wish ... make it comfortable for you ... add furniture ... paint the walls ... hang pictures ... add a window with a view ... add trees, flowers, a sandy beach ... add your personal touches to make it all yours ... and then make yourself comfortable in it.

(PAUSE for 2-3 minutes)

You are the only one who can enter this place unless you invite another in ... no one can hear you ... nothing can distract you ... this is the place where you will meet your self and review your life ... you will, without emotion, see and hear everything you did good and bad, and learn how you could have done better, been more compassionate, expressed more love. You will see those whose lives you touched without knowing.

You may want to invite in your spiritual guides and master teachers to help you in your quest for understanding and enlightenment ... you may want to invite in loved ones who have made their transition before you to help you come to know your self as you truly are. This is where you will learn the importance of forgiveness and gratitude in relationships with other beings ... this is the place where you will begin to remember your spiritual home and your spiritual life that transcends your human experiences ... this is where you will come to know your self and accept your self as you are ... this is where you will let go of your attachments to the physical world and being human ... this is where your consciousness will evolve and take you to higher levels of truth, understanding and wisdom ... this is where you will begin to write your Personal Transition Guidebook to lead you on your journey back to your spiritual home.

Each time you choose to enter this special place and do this inner work, you will be contributing to your spiritual growth and insuring that your transition home is a wondrous experience ... and now silently state your intention and spend some time in this sacred place in the silence of your mind allowing your inner experience to unfold.

(PAUSE for 10-15 minutes)

It will soon be time to leave your sacred place for now, but you will remain in a peaceful relaxed state even after you awaken.

I'm going to count up from 1 to 5 ... with each number you will awaken a little more until I reach the number 5 and you will be fully awake and aware of your surroundings.

One ... you are beginning to come back to an awake state feeling relaxed and refreshed ... you will remember everything you experienced on this journey of self-discovery and your sub-conscious mind will continue to work on it during your daily life and in your dream states ... two ... you are feeling happy and peaceful as if returning from a pleasant trip to a beautiful place ... three ... you feel your self becoming more and more aware of your surroundings, the chair you are sitting in, the room you are in ... four ... you continue to feel lighter, freer, and more relaxed every time you do this exercise ... five ... you are now fully awake and aware of where you are, feeling peaceful and relaxed, calm and happy.

After reading the entire script once for a person, the transition guide may shorten it to just the opening paragraphs or suggest to the person that she go to her Inner Workspace, state her intention and continue with her inner work on her own.

Have the person keep a journal or you keep notes for her about her experiences and use it to help her write her Personal Transition Guidebook.

As a result of this inner work, the person may want to:

- Work on unresolved issues within the family
- Write a gratitude journal
- Write letters with words that need to be said that may be mailed or burned or left to be opened after death, on anniversaries or special occasions
- Make phone calls to say I'm sorry or ask for forgiveness
- Write her Last Will and Advance Directive
- Work on her Bucket List

During medical treatments and procedures, listening to recorded guided visualizations could eliminate anticipatory anxiety, relax the body and engage the mind in other than the procedure going on, or you can participate in it. A guided journey inside one's body can get the patient involved in her own healing by activating her own immune system, white blood cells or T-cells to destroy the alien invader cells.

A transition guide could act as a relaxation coach with a person going through a medical treatment program getting him familiar with the relaxation exercise and using guided visualization to participate in her own healing process. Once you tell the subconscious mind what to do, it will be working to resolve that problem for the highest good of all concerned.

Introducing massage, reiki, light/energy work, acupuncture, aromatherapy, music therapy, and other alternative healing modalities can be a beneficial part of integrative treatment plans by synthesizing the spiritual with the mind and body for more holistic healing.

It's a good time for the transition guide to introduce the practice of conscious dying — because even if the person survives this illness or accident, she will be prepared for the one her body doesn't survive. If this illness kills her body, she will be in control of her transition process.

ొ◦౪

NOTES · NOTES · NOTES · NOTES · NOTES

NOTES · NOTES · NOTES · NOTES · NOTES

Chapter 5

"Death is stripping away all that is not you.
The secret of life is to 'die before you die' —
and find that there is no death."
~ Eckhart Tolle

Why Practice the Art of Conscious Dying

Speaking about death has become a taboo subject in the West, but it's like the elephant in the room. We can continue to ignore it, but everyone knows it's there. So it is important to start a dialog, even with our young children at their level of understanding.

Once we recognize that death is merely part of our journey, not the end of it, it helps to prepare for it as we would any other important event. We can then get on with our lives in a meaningful way, finding our purpose in this life and learning the lessons we came here to learn. What we learn while attending the University of Life on Earth, we take with us upon graduation as we enter the next stage of our eternal lives.

Of course, no one wants to lose a loved one. Most people don't want to die and leave their families. We may not understand but we have to accept it because on the soul level, it makes perfect sense. Death is not a failure or a waste; it is a valuable contribution to the evolution of our consciousness and there are lessons to be learned by everyone involved. This has as much to do with our soul journey as our human lifetimes, which contributes to our spiritual evolution.

We are excited when a new baby is coming into the world. We take birthing classes, we buy furniture and clothes and toys, friends and relatives come to visit bearing gifts, and all eagerly await its entrance into this world.

When it comes to leaving this world, people do not want to talk about it or think about it, no one wants to admit it's going to happen to them, and certainly no one wants to be there when it happens.

Often a dying person is sent off to an end of life care facility to be cared for by strangers or they die alone in a sterile ICU filled with fear and trepidation, while other people make life and death decisions for them.

This leaves everyone with unfinished business. The family goes into a state of shock and disbelief. Each wishes to see the person one more time to tell them something they wish they had told them before they died.

Unfortunately, what they don't realize is that their loved one is there just beyond the veil waiting to hear their words and give them one last embrace before they go.

The one beyond is bewildered because no one prepared him for still being alive after he died and is utterly confused because no one pays any attention to him.

Death is always a loss no matter how you look at it and it doesn't mean there won't be grief, but *what if...?*

- *What if* dying is actually a wonderful, exciting experience as NDErs have described?
- *What if* dying is an opportunity to celebrate the end of a wonderful human experience and a joyous return to our spiritual home and family?
- *What if* death is our graduation from the University of Life on Earth and we go on to have other amazing experiences exploring consciousness at higher levels, being co-creators with God?
- *What if* all those who have transitioned before us are there to greet us, and those we leave behind join us again almost before we know it because there is no time?
- *What if* we exist in a multi-dimensional universe in many different forms in many different frequencies of endless possibilities?
- *What if* consciousness doesn't arise from matter, but creates matter?
- *What if* our True Nature is continuous and our human lifetimes are breathing spaces along our eternal journey?

- *What if* our human lives are not completely predestined and we have the free will to choose to break the cycle of death and rebirth, and move into higher consciousness and higher dimensions?
- *What if* we can accelerate our progress by practicing the art of conscious dying during each human lifetime we experience?
- *What if* we make the spiritual connection in a human lifetime and go directly into the Light at transition, thereby propelling our soul into the next dimension?

How wonderful would that be?

This alternative paradigm offers a whole different way of looking at life — free of the fear of death because we realize there is no death. Anything can happen to my body, but nothing bad can happen to me. Our lives continue on in other realities, in other dimensions. Our bodies die, but each is only one of many our soul manifests then discards.

It's only wishful thinking if all we do is wish, we must be willing to do the work. To accomplish this seems to require that we basically let go of everything and let God — accept that we, the human, are not in control and allow our soul to guide our lives.

This does not mean we have to give up everything, drop out of the world and become monastic. It means letting go of our *attachments* to things, desires, and wants of our egos. Free Will doesn't mean we get to make pigs of ourselves! When we learn to let go and open our consciousness to the Light, all of this information will be revealed to us in this lifetime.

This does not only happen when one has a NDE, but when one goes deep within during meditation and experiences degrees of illumination. When we open the connection between our egoic self/personality and our soul/Higher Self, we experience a down pouring of grace, peace and love. We experience Oneness with All That Is. It is the process of soul healing in action.

Meditation and guided visualization are the basis for practicing conscious dying before we leave our body. If a person at least has that, he may be able to find his way into the Light in case he suddenly finds himself out of his body but still awake.

On the other hand, if you've received a diagnosis that has the potential to be life threatening, this could be your wake up call to include the practice of conscious dying into your holistic health (physical-mental-emotional-spiritual) plan.

Design a workspace in your mind where you can invite in your angels, spirit guides, inner wisdom, healing energy, unconditional love. At some point, healing may not mean stopping the disease process but may bring about a necessary soul healing for which the transition process is the perfect beginning of one's spiritual growth.

In his book, *The Power of Compassion*, The Dalai Lama wrote:

It is during the dream state that we have an opportunity to rehearse or become familiar with the processes of dying, because there is a kind of an analogous process of dissolution experienced during the dream state. In a way, meditators rehearse by utilizing the dream state so that they become familiar with the dissolution processes and train themselves to be able to recognize the various signs that are associated with various levels of dissolution.

But the principle purpose of dream meditation is to train oneself in such a way that, even during the dream state, the individual can actually experience what is known as the Clear Light.

You already know this. You've simply forgotten. Being born into the physical world does that to us — makes us forget that we are essentially spiritual beings here as part of our greater spiritual journey. It's like going away for a semester to study abroad. It is only the attractions and distractions of the physical world that cause us to turn our attention and forget which reality is real. Dying is actually waking up!

So now perhaps you're remembering — that there is more to you than you think you are, than you've been led to believe — that other people have defined who you are, told you what to do, how to think and who to be. You believed them because you have forgotten who you really are. By remembering, you're breaking free of being controlled and out of control.

When something you read or hear suddenly makes perfect sense, it is because it triggered the memory of what you already knew. You had to see it in a new light to recognize it, to really feel the truth of it.

Every light bulb moment you have while reading this book, will be a remembrance of a spiritual teaching you forgot you knew or a soul memory surfacing, calling for your attention — reminding you that you are on a spiritual path and it's time to make some changes in your lifestyle and your thought patterns for the healing of your soul.

Now that you're starting to remember, you'll want to start thinking about writing your own Personal Transition Guidebook to remind you about the path you want to take when it is your time to prepare yourself to return to your spiritual home.

If you are a caregiver for a loved one reading this, learning the art of conscious dying will help you initiate meaningful conversations among family members that will provide comfort for all involved. As you guide your loved one through his life review, and facilitate forgiveness and gratitude sessions with family members, old wounds can be healed and new bonds may be created.

The family can even be prepared for after-death communications that will help with the grief process. Instead of moaning about not being there to say goodbye, they will know to be still and listen with an open heart and an open mind for the presence of their loved one. They can prepare a place for the deceased members at family celebrations because they know that even those who are not in body are still with them.

The Journey From the Inside Out of Body

If one's body has been deteriorating over time whether from old age or a progressive disease process and you are approaching death awareness, and if you are practicing conscious dying, you are likely no longer concerned about your body.

At some point, even days before you leave your body, you may become very contemplative, deeply exploring this inner world that has been emerging in your consciousness through your practice of conscious dying. You may lose interest in what goes on in the external world and become quite sensitive to strong odors, bright lights and loud noises.

Good advice for loved ones and caregivers is to approach you gently, talk softly, leave TVs and radios off, and close the windows and doors if it tends to be noisy outside. If you want your favorite music playing or the services of a music thanatologist (usually a harpist), let your loved ones know.

Those around you need to be aware that your deathing room is a sacred space and you don't want to be interrupted while visiting the other side.

If you have been practicing the art of conscious dying, you have prepared yourself to accelerate your progress along your transition journey and are getting ready to move on.

Dying people will often linger and observers wonder why they are hanging on, why they don't let go. Several things could be going on. They may be enjoying the experience so much they are not ready to let go. They may be so afraid, they can't let go. They may still be so attached to their body/life they won't let go. Or they could be involved in their life review, working through some stubborn old past life karma that they really want to cut loose in this life.

Those who appear to be struggling in the physical world may be having a hard time letting go of erroneous beliefs or fears long held in consciousness.

Those who have prepared themselves for this journey by letting go and opening their hearts to unconditional love, and practicing with their Personal Transition Guidebook, may have no trouble letting go when they realize what they have been experiencing in their meditations matches their experience of shifting back and forth between dimensions as they are dying.

Even if one's body has become immobile, you can still cross yourself over consciously using the meditative practice you developed using your Guidebook. Having someone read your Guidebook as you make your transition can be most helpful to keep you focused on the path you want to take. If you have slipped into a coma, you will continue to hear the voice of the person reading your Guidebook.

As your body is dying, your organs are shutting down and your soul is withdrawing from a body it no longer needs. In consciousness, you may be experiencing flashes of light, feelings of shrinking then expanding, spinning, floating, familiar and unfamiliar images surrounding you, complete silence, thunderous sounds, or complete bliss and freedom, as this shutting down process unfolds.

You can write these symptoms into your Guidebook so you will be reminded that they are just part of the process — you may notice them but there's no need to pay attention to them. Just observe them and then let them go.

Your actual experience may depend on:
• The energy you bring with you

- Your last thoughts and feelings at the moment of your body's death
- The level of consciousness at which you lived your life
- Where your thoughts dwelled most frequently
- The love and compassion you expressed to others
- The random acts of kindness you performed

These determine the frequency at which your energy will vibrate on the other side. It is not a moral judgment about your life or behaviors. During your life review you will be faced with the times in your life when you could have done better as part of your soul's education.

You can't hide from your soul but God is all about Unconditional Love. There is no wrath or eternal punishment to fear. Any images that might arise are mental images within your own consciousness and you can choose which to pay attention to.

In the early twilight stage, the dying person may be simultaneously experiencing consciousness in two dimensions. He may drift back and forth from the physical dimension to the spiritual dimension, letting go of one, adjusting to the other, as if he has become a balloon, floating effortlessly on his thought waves. His awareness of what is expands beyond the limits of his physical senses and he begins remembering all that he had forgotten when he became a human.

He may be having a conversation with his loved ones on the other side and then his consciousness drifts back to his body in the bed where his loved ones on this side are relieved to see him lucid again in their presence.

The dying one does not notice there is a difference

because it is all happening in the present moment. Those on this side may think he is delusional, but he may be communicating with those on the other side because in his expanding awareness, there is no other side.

When a person has worked with a transition guide, he will be hearing her reading his Personal Transition Guidebook. He will be able to focus on the words and not be distracted by any mental images that may arise in his awareness.

The words he wrote in his Guidebook are to remind him that these are products of his own imagination — they are not real. He has left his body and no-*thing* can harm him.

The goal of practicing the art of conscious dying is to process all this information by doing life reviews through meditation and guided visualization before one makes his transition so he doesn't have to be confronted with them on the other side. This prepares him to recognize his True Nature immediately as the Clear Light dawns and take a huge leap toward his soul's goal of achieving God-Consciousness.

Unless a person realizes all of this on his own, he is likely to miss *this life's* opportunity to achieve freedom for his soul to move on to higher dimensions. This soul may quickly reincarnate to try again or spend some time on the other side healing from the misadventures of this lifetime before choosing to have another go.

It also may be that a soul is not prepared to evolve to God-Consciousness during this lifetime regardless of what the human self (ego/personality) thinks or wants. Or it may be that a certain amount of awareness developed in this lifetime will enable a soul to consciously evolve during its next incarnation and achieve liberation at the moment of the death of that body.

I've heard people say *I'm never coming back here again* or *this is my last lifetime,* but on the other side, souls are clamoring for another opportunity to reincarnate. It makes a big difference when we realize there is a purpose for all of this and that we have some control over the outcome.

We live many, many lifetimes as different human beings facing different relationships and experiences, learning the lessons our souls need to learn at the University of Life on Earth. Each lifetime is important to our spiritual growth and to the evolution of consciousness of humanity.

We, as human beings, are becoming conscious of ourselves as *whole* beings, *both* Human *and* Divine... and we are learning to adapt to that situation!

Processing Forgiveness and Gratitude

Letting go of guilt and fear, and by forgiving others and opening our heart to Love, brings us closer to God.
~ Course in Miracles

Besides not remembering that we are actually Beings of Light experiencing lifetimes as conscious biological beings existing in a physical dimension, the biggest obstacle to a peaceful transition experience is failure to reconcile one's life (dissolve karma) before transition.

The life review NDErs talk about shows us the times in our lives that we were not being loving, kind or compassionate as well as the times we were. It is not a judgment by an authoritarian God/King figure resulting in an eternal sentence to heaven or hell as some religions have interpreted it. It is a teaching about what it means to live in harmony with The Universe, Mother Nature and other life forms as a Divine Human Being.

As humans, we have forgotten about our true spiritual nature. We think we are alone on this rock, an accidental creature with no future and no accountability. We see earth as our playground and think we can do anything we want to it without it having any effect upon anyone or anything else.

We often see human beings outside our family, tribe, community or nation as intruders, enemies, insignificant others, evildoers, infidels somehow not worthy of our love or respect.

This attitude has led us to condone starvation, torture, war, genocide, rape, stoning, kidnapping and polluting our environment without regard to the effects on our own consciousness or other life forms on the planet. Not only do we have our own personal karma to account for during a life review, but global karma as well.

It has taken this many lifetimes for human beings to begin to realize we are all one. We are one with each other, one with the planet, one with the cosmos, one with the Source of our being. One Consciousness — just as a wave or drop of water is one with the ocean.

Everything we do as individual human beings affects everyone and everything else because we are connected, we are one; therefore it starts with each individual to bring about change — a change in personal and global consciousness. To do this we need to practice forgiveness and gratitude with compassion; first in our own lives and with ourselves, then outward into the world.

As part of the practice of conscious dying, we can use guided visualization to seek out those in our lives whom we need to forgive and those who need our forgiveness — not for their sakes, but for our own.

We don't need to confront a person directly, although it may be more powerful to do so, but it is not always possible or advisable. It can be done symbolically, but it is best done before transition. Carrying it with us when we go will hold us back.

We need to forgive ourselves for being hateful, angry, vengeful, or jealous and understand that these thoughts and behaviors are related to lessons we came into body to learn. We need to forgive others for their behaviors toward us and wish them well on their own spiritual paths to clear our own conscience.

Holding onto these feelings only hurts those who do. Held inside, they can cause physical symptoms and emotional disturbances until we understand the connection between mind and body, and shift our perspective toward healing.

By doing this we are not condoning other people's bad behaviors, we are letting go of the burden of carrying around (internalizing) the feelings of anger or resentment toward them. As we practice dying consciously, we learn to release these feelings, first by forgiving our self for giving away our power, health, love; second, by forgiving the person and thanking their soul for agreeing to come into this life as a teacher to us on our spiritual path. He will learn his lessons during his own life review. We are all students as well as teachers to each other, depending on the circumstances.

This reminds me of the story about the two monks who were traveling in silence through a forest to their monastery when they came upon a woman who was carrying a basket of food from the market and looking to find a place to cross a rushing stream. When she asked for help, one monk picked her up and carried her across the stream.

Many hours later the silent monks reached their destination. At the entrance, one monk turned to the other and said in an angry tone, "You should not have picked that woman up. We are not supposed to touch a female body." The other monk said, "I put that woman down hours ago and you are still carrying her around in your head."

The same goes for gratitude. We can't thank people in our lives that are important to us enough times. There are people who played significant roles in our lives that we never really thanked — parents, teachers, friends, strangers. Appreciation expressed brings the love in your heart out into your energy field and radiates outward to touch others. It's the Ripple Effect.

Many people take a lot of things for granted as if they are entitled — food in a refrigerator, a roof over our heads, clothes on our back, clean running water, flush toilets, a car to drive, money in the bank, a free education, a peaceful lifestyle. Many people have none of these things and are grateful for every morsel of food, drop of water, and moment of rest from the burden of obtaining it.

When we are dying, these memories from our past begin to come back to us — like bubbles arising in consciousness that awaken a forgotten memory. NDErs tell us that while out of body they experienced a life review not just as an observer but as if they were in the experience, feeling their own feelings and the feelings of the other people involved in situations that happened in their lives. They were shown kindnesses they did and the ripple effect, as well as their unkindnesses and the repercussions to others.

It's only upon stepping out of the frame and seeing the whole picture that we get the lesson the situation was showing us. It is helpful to our soul growth to get the lesson before we make our transition — in life review work as we practice dying consciously.

A person can get started on his life review by processing forgiveness and gratitude issues before his actual transition time. He may enter his inner workspace and use guided visualization techniques to clear the blockages caused by living in denial, being unable to forgive, holding onto old hurts and anger, and not letting go of addictions to the physical world.

Clearing the Chakras is a good guided visualization script to start the process and pairing the memory of an event with the energy center affected will open up the energy center. This is a method to raise one's vibration to meet the highest frequency of Light during transition. The more unnecessary baggage you can dump before transition, the *lighter* you will be!

Questions to Ask Your Higher Self

The following are some questions you may want to meditate on to help you develop a plan to prepare yourself for whatever may come. Some of these questions, you may never have thought about before and you may need to do some deep spiritual searching to be able to answer them. Meditate on one question at a time for as long as you are able.

There are no "correct" answers; just write down whatever comes to you — this is your truth. Just start writing even if it doesn't make sense, a word, a phrase, babble. Come back to it later and play with the words some more. Your answers may determine the early course of your journey and the words you write in your Personal Transition Guidebook to remind you where you want to be going.

- *Who am I, really?*
- *What do I really believe?*
- *What are my values?*
- *What are my addictions?*
- *How has my religion or belief system sustained or failed me through my life?*
- *What happens to me after my body dies?*
- *What does it mean to die?*
- *Describe what life in an after life might be like.*
- *What is the meaning of life?*
- *What is my soul's purpose?*

- *Describe God in your own words.*
- *What question would you ask God?*
- *Have you ever had a spiritual experience you couldn't explain or deny?*
- *Why is the universe the way it is?*
- *Why is there anything at all?*
- *What do you fear?*
- *Why do we even have thoughts? Who is the thinker?*
- *Have I lived the life I've always wanted to live?*
- *Did I love unconditionally?*
- *Do I have any regrets? Anger? Resentments?*
- *Is there anyone I haven't forgiven?*
- *What is it like to live with a terminal illness or knowing you are going to die soon?*
- *What do you still need to feel mentally, emotionally and spiritually ready for your transition?*
- *How do you want your family to remember you?*
- *What are the last things you want to say to your loved ones?*
- *What message do you want written on your tombstone?*

Re-reading your responses again will help you sort out your thinking so you'll know how to proceed. You may want to make a prioritized list of things you want to do or accomplish or finish before you die (your "Bucket List) — a list of people you need to forgive or repay or express gratitude, as well as things you want to do before you can't.

Judgment or Healing

As the Ancient Egyptian God of the Underworld Anubis (a large imposing jackal-headed figure with a male human body) weighed the heart of the departed against Truth, represented by an ostrich feather, on a scale to determine the person's worthiness to enter the After Life, as depicted in hieroglyphics on the walls of tombs and pyramids, one's heart must be light in order to match the frequency of the Clear Light and merge with it.

It's not that they were wrong, it's just that those jackal-headed guys reflected their reality at the time and appear a bit far-fetched to modern day people, but the idea is the same. It all boils down to we reap what we sow.

Some religious traditions claim there is a judgment of one's life before one can enter the Kingdom of Heaven or that souls lie asleep awaiting a Final Judgment at the end of the world. Some NDErs do have a "religious" experience where they may meet Jesus or another religious figure but most do not. Religions are based on human imaginations trying to explain what is unexplainable, just as near-death experiences are said to be ineffable.

Most contemporary NDErs report that we are accountable to ourselves. We can't hide anything from our soul, all is revealed during a life review. Also there is no rest in peace! There is soul work to be done! For some it's healing or assisting others. For others, it's further learning, exploring and understanding the workings of the energy in the physical universe and other dimensions. Our "jobs" on higher levels involve maintaining and co-creating "life" in the physical dimensions.

NDErs report experiencing unconditional love and acceptance regardless of their religious beliefs. Even atheists come back with changed perceptions. Exposure to this Light has changed hardened criminals into messengers of God's Unconditional Love and ordinary people into volunteers in service to humanity. Even a frightening or hellish experience turns out to be purifying and loving.

If you are learning this before you are close to dying, you are learning to let go of your emotional baggage instead of carrying it around all your life then trying to let go of it all a few days before you leave your body.

Guided visualization is a tool for releasing these feelings before they become attachments, addictions or distractions. This is something you can learn to do yourself — a periodic life review to release things as they come up; however, talking about it with a therapist or spiritual counselor may be more therapeutic.

Your life review guided visualizations will provide the framework to write your Personal Transition Guidebook and will help you reach acceptance of your own death, whether you have a terminal diagnosis, are elderly, or are perfectly healthy, young and enjoying life. It becomes part of planning for your life, like retirement.

Once you have a good grasp of your belief system, your views on the afterlife, and the meaning of your life, you can begin to design your transitional journey from your own perspective and put it into the form of your Personal Transition Guidebook.

৯০৵

NOTES · NOTES · NOTES · NOTES · NOTES

NOTES · NOTES · NOTES · NOTES · NOTES

_____

_____

_____

_____

_____

_____

_____

_____

_____

_____

_____

_____

_____

_____

_____

_____

_____

_____

_____

_____

Chapter 6

> "Thou wilt pay undistracted attention to that
> with which I am about to set thee face to face,
> and hold on; O nobly-born,
> that which is called death hath now come."
> ~ The Bardol Thodol

Books of the Dead

It's not just in modern times that people have described their visions of the afterlife. These experiences have been written about in stories and songs, and have been the basis of most religions for thousands of years.

Over 5,000 years ago, the Ancient Egyptians wrote funerary texts in hieroglyphics on papyrus scrolls (See *Appendix* for description), and later painted their

Book of the Dead glyphs on the walls of the tombs and pyramids of their pharaohs and dignitaries as a guidebook, providing spells, incantations and keys to help the deceased navigate through the Underworld to get to the After Life.

The Tibetans, isolated from the rest of the world atop the Himalayas for centuries, using their knowledge of life in between lives gleaned from experiences deep in mediation, developed *The Bardo Thodol: Liberation through Hearing in the Intermediate State* (See *Appendix* for excerpt). They had an understanding about hearing continuing after the death of the body from earlier near-death experiencers. The text is read to a dying or dead person to guide the soul through the 49 Days of the Bardo to achieve either liberation from the cycle of life, death and rebirth or toward a successful rebirth.

Ars Moriendi, The Art of Dying Well, according to Christian precepts, was conceived of during medieval times when the bubonic plague wiped out millions of people, including many priests who attended to the sick and dying. Lay people were given instructions in, and the authority to administer Last Rites to aid the dying during their transition. Reaffirming faith, repenting for one's sins and letting go of worldly possessions and desires were important. The stages of dying, temptations to avoid, rules of behavior, questions to ask the dying, and so on were depicted on woodcuts; all instructions for having a "good death."

Most modern religions have some form of end of life rituals, usually read by a priest or minister, to prepare the person for dying by affirming their beliefs, asking forgiveness, atoning for sins, and saying prayers in hopes of being accepted into the heavenly realms based on their beliefs. These rites all come about through the interpretations of ineffable experiences into other dimensions of God/Source by humans of varying levels of understanding and consciousness. Each only had his own small window into Infinity.

Just as in the poem, "The Blind Men and the Elephant" (see *Appendix*), they are different interpretations of the same experience or parts of a greater unseen whole.

Writing Your Personal Transition Guidebook

The Personal Transition Guidebook is not a book that is already written like *The Tibetan Book of the Dead*. It is not based on any one religion or theology. It is a very personal document, which one writes for her self, using words and phrases that are meaningful to her, often with the assistance of a transition guide. A transition guide can be helpful by being objective, and providing information and suggestions from this handbook.

A Personal Transition Guidebook includes the method one develops through practicing to forgive, to let go, to release, to merge with the Light. It may include statements of forgiveness to all those who have hurt you or whom you have hurt releasing them to their highest good. You can send love to all your loved ones or all sentient beings. You can surround any negative energy you might encounter with love and light. You can thank all those who loved and supported you, and your soul for the opportunity to live this lifetime together. It is your journey and needs to be written in your own words, based on your own beliefs and perspectives about your personal transition process.

If you follow a religion, use those familiar words to make it more real for you. Use your favorite scriptures, quotations, stories, or hymns. If you don't follow a religion, use your imagination to describe your ideas about this transformational journey to another dimension.

Write it as if you are writing about your odyssey from one land to another as you imagine it will be. Design it in your own mind during your meditations. Be as detailed in description as you want. You may want to include:

- Poetry, scripture, stories
- Meetings with your loved ones on the other side
- Expressions of love to those you are leaving behind
- Encounters with your guides, your angels, Jesus, God, Allah, Buddha
- Feeling surrounded by unconditional love and acceptance
- Merging with the Clear Light

Remind yourself that this experience takes place in consciousness and no-*thing* can harm you; that all is for your highest good. Continually remind yourself to let go of the physical world and go into the Light.

The sample script that follows will give you some ideas to help you get started. Part 1, which is read before physical death and immediately afterwards, should describe the transition process as the person expects to be experiencing it in the language of her beliefs. The words remind the personality/ego to let go of its attachments to the physical body and the physical world, to rise above it, to say one's final goodbyes and to look for the Clear

Light of Ultimate Reality.

Remind the dying person to ignore any distractions (mental images that may arise in consciousness), to let go of physical desires, and continue seeking the Light. If the person has worked through her life review process, made amends, forgiven and asked for forgiveness, expressed gratitude and reconciled her life before death, Part 1 should be sufficient to guide her into the Light.

If a person has been unwilling or hasn't taken the time to resolve unpleasant issues in her life before her transition, she may need more assistance with letting go of her attachments to the physical world.

Part 2 is designed to help the person dissolve the karma/energy that keeps her stuck on the physical plane and its distractions, and recognize the Secondary Light when it dawns. The reading of Part 2 may begin a half hour after death and be read occasionally for several days after death.

In the case of a close friend or relative, the transition guide may be aware of the issues the person has been unable to let go of and they may have written a Part 2 just to cover all bases. This is where the transition guide's intuition comes in. He may be able to sense that the soul is struggling or when it has let go.

A highly sensitive guide, including those who are NDErs, may be able to follow a person's soul to the other side and make sure she goes to the Light, may even be able to bring back a message upon their return to those at the bedside. Dr. Raymond Moody, in his recent book, *Glimpses of Eternity: Sharing a Loved Ones Passage From This Life to the Next,* has reported such cases and

I have experienced this as well with a number of my hospice patients.

The Tibetan Book of the Dead offers four parts, with 3 and 4 being reserved to guide the most corrupt, reprehensible, unscrupulous, malicious human beings to seek the Tertiary Light and will not be described here as these people would require a professional Transition Guide's expertise.

According to the Tibetans, freedom from karma and recognizing one's Self in the Clear Light leads to Liberation from the Cycle of Life, Death and Rebirth. The Secondary Light offers the soul healing and respite from rebirth, and further education toward spiritual growth before planning another sojourn into a physical world. The Tertiary Light offers immediate rebirth for a soul that needs to continue working on karmic lessons.

However, it's not the transition guide's place to decide for anyone what she should expect much beyond leaving her body, saying goodbye to loved ones and seeking the Light. This is where NDE stories diverge and the individual's religious beliefs come in. Those must be respected no matter what the transition guide believes.

NDErs who have written about their experiences have provided a variety of descriptions and experiences, as well as enough similar experiences to provide possible scenarios. I suggest reading Josie Varga's book, *Visits to Heaven,* and going online to Dr. Jeffrey Long's web site, NDERF.org to read NDE stories to get some ideas about what you hope your journey will be like. If one has a strong belief system, it is likely she will experience what she expects at first and her Guidebook should reflect those beliefs.

If the person isn't coherent or able to communicate, a close relative or friend should help with the writing of her guidebook so that it is about the dying person and not the transition guide.

Practicing Your Personal Transition Guidebook

Why would one need a guidebook to get to the other side? Haven't human beings been dying for tens of thousands of years? Well, yes, but it seems the problem is most of us aren't getting it right and it's holding humanity back in spiritual development which is reflected in the outer turmoil in this world. We seem to be stuck in a space-time warp!

Anthony Borgia, a spiritualist psychic who received messages from Monsignor Robert Hugh Benson in response to questions, wrote:

> *I think if one were asked what was the most common mental state in which the majority of people arrive in the spirit world, I should be disposed to reply from a fairly extensive experience, that they arrive in a state of bewilderment and complete ignorance of the fact that they have passed from the earth world.*

It seems the problem is that many people aren't prepared for their return to the spiritual world because they are afraid this physical lifetime is all there is — and then nothing. They assume or believe that when we die, it's lights out, life is over and we'll never see our loved ones again.

Maybe that's why so many people are having NDEs these days, so we can let others know that our experiences are real and the secret they reveal is that WE DO NOT DIE! Only our physical body dies.

We are not our bodies. We are not our personalities, our emotions, our jobs, what we have or don't have. We are in the world, but not of it. Who we are is Pure Consciousness in physical form.

When Pure Consciousness manifested the physical universe and it evolved into physical systems capable of supporting biological life forms that evolved into beings capable of survival and conscious evolution, the resulting humans lost awareness of themselves as *spiritual* beings having experiences in *physical* bodies with similar and compatible others.

We have forgotten we are Pure Consciousness experiencing a physical, biological aspect of ourself through our human eyes, brain and other senses, communicating with and loving each other, expressing joy for each other and being on this beautiful planet together for a brief moment.

As human beings, we get to share in this glorious adventure with other life forms plus have a vacation on a beautiful, bountiful planet and attend the University of Life on Earth. The goal in a single human lifetime is to remember this while still in body to attain enlightenment and ascend directly into the Light by our own free will. Practicing the art of conscious dying before one's body dies is a way to access higher consciousness and achieve that goal prior to physical death. We are able to wake up and remember what we forgot at birth.

Understanding the process of transition from the physical world to the spiritual world of light and transfiguration from our physical body to our spiritual form of light is the foundation of the Personal Transition Guidebook, which you will write to keep you on track while it is happening.

However you envision your journey during your meditations and guided visualizations is the journey you want to practice before you leave your body so that when you do, you have some tools to help you through the process. In the past, tools have been described as spells, incantations, passwords, keys to open doors to guide the soul through the Underworld, the Bardo, Purgatory, to get to Ra or Zeus or God or the Light. They all may work; they just need to be practiced before they are needed.

Otherwise, we may suddenly wake up one day in a strange but familiar environment. We can see our earthly family but they can't see us. We can see our spiritual family but we are confused. We can't wrap our mind around what has happened right away. It's cognitive dissonance times the Power of 10. We don't know where to go or what to do. Our first reaction may be fear and resistance to what's happening, and we may try to go back to what is known or familiar to us, which is quite frustrating when no one responds to our frantic attempts to communicate.

The reader of your Guidebook will be there to keep you on your path to the Light during your transition experience. The practice of it with the transition guide reading aloud is to teach the dying person to keep her attention on the reader's familiar voice so she is not distracted by any negative thought-forms remaining in her energy field as her soul leaves her body.

If you write your Guidebook well in advance of the death of your body, read it occasionally throughout your life to keep the content fresh in your mind. Reading or having someone read your Guidebook to you every day during the weeks and days as you prepare to step out of your body will help keep you focused during the days and nights leading up to it.

When your loved ones have been prepared beforehand, are familiar with your Guidebook, and are at your side supporting your transition with their love/light/energy, all involved may experience an overwhelming infusion of love as you leave your body, say your last goodbyes, and merge peacefully with the Light.

As previously discussed, there are two ways to exit your body: suddenly, with little to no warning; or slowly, over time. Slowly is a relative term, which could mean the next day after an accident or 20 years after one receives an initial diagnosis.

The best time to begin the practice of conscious dying might be the same time you get your first driver's license because as teenagers we are the most vulnerable to sudden death for the next 10 years. Perhaps it should be taught in high school, certainly before boys and girls are sent off to war.

The thing is we need to learn about it before our body dies because we don't know when that may happen. Some bodies do die young and without warning. Many people still don't want to consider the possibility and think the whole idea of talking about it is just plain morbid or forbidden or frightening.

One person went as far as to tell me that encouraging a dying person to let go was like murdering them. These are the people most shocked and grief-stricken when someone they love dies. They can't understand how God could be so cruel and are angry at the unfairness of it all when God has nothing to do with it and, on the soul level, all is in Divine Order.

It is often not until there is a death in the family that people begin to examine their beliefs and start a search for meaning. Introducing this loving practice of reconciliation and conscious dying may lead to greater openness within the family. When dying is considered an integral part of life, essential to one's spiritual growth and conscious evolution, people are free to be more open with their feelings and compassionate toward others. They are able to express their questions and concerns about death, dying, and the afterlife and re-examine their belief system. They are able to put their lives in perspective and the family is able to be supportive.

With the shared realization that we don't die, we simply expand our energy beyond our physical form, cut it loose and move on to the next developmental stage of existence, we are all able to help each other deal with our shared loss and grief over the temporary separation caused by the death of the body.

Celebrations of Life become earth-family traditions of honoring the graduation from the University of Life on Earth of another beloved soul-family member. The family gathered around the bedside raising their vibrations to midwife the soul to the loved ones and healers waiting on the other side to carry her home, is a picture needing to be painted. Personal Transition Guidebooks from deceased family members can become tools for the new family members to learn about their predecessors, and their thoughts about physical death and the afterlife.

Reading Your
Personal Transition Guidebook

The sample script scenario is written for a person who believes life goes on after death and has prepared himself according to his understanding of the process of conscious dying into the Light. It may not relate to the reader's belief system but it can easily be adapted to any more or less religious belief system. I've used the word "God" but readers may substitute whatever name they are comfortable with when it appears in the text.

The first phase of the journey may begin for the dying person hours before the breath ceases and continue for about twenty minutes after for the average person — one with little-to-some spiritual awareness. It will be over in a flash for one with a highly evolved consciousness during physical life, and last much longer than twenty minutes for those who are spiritually unconscious — with little-to-no belief in a Higher Power or an afterlife at the time of their death.

Where a person is on this consciousness continuum may be determined through conversation with the person or family members if there is time before death approaches. People may be more willing to talk about dying as death comes nearer and after they have reached acceptance. If they are working with a transition guide, they are likely to be open to fascinating conversations.

The place for the transition guide is at the dying person's side, near his head, so he can hear the early instructions clearly. The transition guide may watch for the signs of approaching death and keep the dying person aware that the Clear Light will be dawning shortly by reading softly aloud.

Signs for the transition guide to watch for are:
• Relaxing facial muscles
• Labored or erratic breathing
• Glazed eyes
• Blueness beneath the fingernails
• Extreme coldness and blueness in the feet that gradually creeps up the legs

When the reading begins, others in the room will be radiating loving energy to uplift the soul and mentally concentrating on helping the dying person raise his frequency to match the Light.

The transition guide will need to rely on her intuition to know where the soul is in the process of spiritual rebirth, just as an experienced obstetrician senses where the baby is in the birth canal. This is a tool that can be developed and for those not naturally intuitive or empathic, classes and tapes are available online to help one develop that ability.

As the time of death nears, as determined by physical and vital signs, begin to repeat the signals of the approaching Clear Light to keep the person focused and remind them that the sensations she is experiencing are normal and there is nothing to fear. Those who have achieved acceptance of their death are likely to be more peaceful at this stage.

The voice of the transition guide is a gentle reminder in the background. Listen to what a dying person is able to tell you about what he is experiencing and be supportive.

He may not be so much confused as he is amazed!

Allow the dying person periods of silence (between read paragraphs) so he can be present with his experience as his consciousness shifts back and forth. Read to him and express loving thoughts to him whether he is lucid in the physical world or seemingly unconscious. Continue reading and during pauses use your mental energy to direct him to the Clear White Light.

The person's favorite scriptures or other religious readings, prayers, or poems, may be read by the transition guide, family members, friends, a minister, to keep the departing soul focused on his transition, letting go and moving into the Light.

As consciousness begins to expand, the mature emotional atom departs from the body. To those in attendance, it may appear the person has entered a coma, however his consciousness has not ceased. His hearing is still active. As the mature mental atom withdraws, consciousness expands beyond the veil. The heartbeat slows considerably as awareness withdraws from the body/brain and observes its physical form from above.

The heart will still be beating as the Clear Light begins to dawn and the words of the transition guide will help him hold to the Light as his soul drifts further away from his body. Coldness around the heart signifies cessation of the heartbeat and departure of the mature heart atom.

Experiencing Your Inner Journey

As death approaches, pain meds may be lowered or discontinued if the person is comfortable and wants to remain awake during his transition process. The person's emotions drop away as he finds himself letting go of his attachments to the physical world (the room he is in, the loved ones around him, the life he lived) and becoming more involved in the wonder and awe of his more frequent glimpses beyond the veil.

Though his awareness may shift back and forth for some time (days or hours), he will continue to "hear" what goes on around his body telepathically, even after his body would be considered dead. That doesn't mean he will respond, as he will be quite busy with leaving his physical body and adjusting to his new awareness. Some dying people may be able to describe what they are seeing or experiencing even up to the last breath.

The first sensations he may experience indicating the process is beginning, may be of becoming smaller and smaller — a mental experience of shrinking downward. At the same time, the person may lose control of his body's muscle tension and feel himself sinking into the bed. He may experience difficulty swallowing and not want food or water. He may appear to relax and become peaceful to observers.

At any time, he may begin to hear snapping or popping noises. These are the sounds of the threads of the etheric cord breaking. There is no pain involved at any time during this transition process.

During the next stage, the person may experience alternating sensations of cold and heat. He may experience chills, chattering teeth and shivering followed by extreme irritability or agitation. These are the affects of light energy rising up the spinal column, via the Chakras, and exiting the physical body.

If the person prepared himself by practicing dying consciously for this moment, he may be working with the energy, directing it upwards through his Chakras and out the top of his head or Crown Chakra.

This is where the inner forgiveness and gratitude work done previously contribute to raising one's vibration as consciousness leaves the body to reunite with the soul. If this work hasn't been done, the life force may leave through another Chakra point taking those unreleased emotions with it to be dealt with during the life review on the other side.

The next sensation the dying person may experience is as if he is expanding and about to burst. As his consciousness moves out of his physical body, his vibratory rate increases to match the frequency of his departing energy.

His breathing may become very labored. There may be panting as in giving birth. He may be hearing buzzing noises, high-pitched whistling, or low rolling thunder. He may feel a band of pressure around his head as if his head is about to explode. At the same time, he may be feeling exhilarated.

His feet and hands may feel tingly, as if they have

gone to sleep. He may alternate between hot and cold. His body may feel fluid, like melting wax. He may begin to experience visions, distorted images that rise and fade away in his awareness.

Lastly, he may feel a vibration starting at the base of the spine, rising upward along the spinal column, reaching toward the head. As the physical brain shuts down, conscious awareness suddenly expands beyond the physical dimension.

He may smile, may even sit up in bed, and try to explain to those in attendance that he has just seen God or heaven or deceased relatives or angels singing him home — and then his body will fall back onto the bed, his heart will stop beating and his wondrous rebirth journey into the spiritual world will commence according to his spiritual path.

NOTES · NOTES · NOTES · NOTES · NOTES

Personal Transition Guidebook

(Sample)

PART 1

(To be read while person is actively dying and for about 20 minutes after their last breath)

Focus your attention on the sound of my voice.

Listen to the words I am saying.

These are your words and they are reassuring you that you know where you are and where you are going.

You are aware that your physical life is nearly over and you are in the process of letting go of your attachments to your body and the material world.

Your mind is at peace.

Whatever sensations you are experiencing are normal.

There is no-thing to fear.

You may feel yourself becoming smaller and smaller... shrinking into a black velvet void.

Your muscles are relaxing more and more with each exhale as your breathing slows ... and the spaces between breaths grow longer and longer.

You feel more and more peaceful with each breath.

You feel more and more peaceful in between each breath.

You feel more and more peaceful ... relaxed ... filled with a gentle anticipation.

You feel lighter and lighter as you let go more and more.

You may feel as if you are sinking into the bed, a big feather bed as soft as a cloud.

You feel surrounded by love.

You feel loved.

You feel your beloved surrounding you with love.

You are letting go of the physical world and spending more and more time visiting the spiritual world that appears around you.

You feel so loved, so accepted, so right, as you let go more and more.

You may find yourself looking for the light but so much is happening you find it difficult to concentrate.

Focus on the sound of my voice.

Listen to my voice as I speak your words.

You may be hearing snapping or popping noises.

These are signs that your soul is pulling away from your body ... gradually withdrawing the life force from the body and returning it to your soul.

Any pain you felt before has faded away as you become less aware of your body and more aware of the spiritual body you are building with the love you gave to others during your human life.

If you have any regrets or grievances or unresolved issues from your human lifetime, this is your final opportunity to make amends before you carry these attachments with you on your spiritual journey.

Now is the time to let go.

Now is the time to forgive.

Now is the time to seek forgiveness.

Now is the time to see yourself as you really are.

Now is the time to be your true self.

You are letting go of all desire for food and drink.

You are letting go of your attachments to things of the material world.

You are letting go of your need for power and control. [or appropriate negative patterns]

You are letting go of your needs for self-gratification.

You are letting go of your loved ones on this side knowing that you will see them again.

You are letting go of your physical body.

You are letting go of who you thought you were and seeing yourself as you truly are.

You are remembering you have been a spiritual being all along.

You are remembering you are returning home once again.

You are remembering you are both human and divine.

You are taking with you all the love you experienced.

You are taking with you all the love you gave to others.

You are taking with you all the love others gave to you.

You are taking with you every sunrise and sunset you ever watched.

You are taking with you every flower you ever admired.

You are taking with you every joyful moment you experienced.

You are taking with you the joy of every accomplishment you ever achieved.

You are taking with you every song you ever sang.

You are taking with you every kind word you ever expressed and every kind deed you did selflessly.

You are anticipating the joy of returning to your spiritual home and your spiritual family filled with love and peace.

You are feeling higher vibrations around you and within you.

You may experience alternating sensations of cold and heat.

You may experience chills, chattering teeth, shivering followed by sweating.

You may feel agitated and restless.

There is no-thing to fear.

You are experiencing your light energy moving from the base of your spine toward the top of your head.

Focus on the light moving upward.

Move the energy with your thoughts ... upward, upward.

Imagine bright lights turning on as the light energy passes through each energy point of your body.

At the base of your spine ... red.

At the navel ... orange.

At the solar plexus ... yellow.

At the heart ... green

At the throat ... blue.

At the third eye ... indigo.

At the crown of the head ... purple.

As each color turns on, feel yourself letting go of your attachments to those vibrations.

As you see each color turn on, feel yourself letting go of negative emotions and rising above your physical body.

Stay with each color as long as you need to in order to let go completely of anything holding you back.

As you work the energy up toward your head centers, your vibratory rate increases ... you are filled with joy... a warm loving energy surrounds you.

Once the purple light clears, you will begin to see into the pure White Light of the spiritual dimension.

In this loving Light, you will see your previously deceased relatives waiting to welcome you on the other side.

At the same time, you will still be able to see the loved ones at your bedside and you may be able to communicate to them what you are seeing, hearing and feeling during your transition journey.

You may be seeing your body lying in a bed from above your body.

You may be able to be at the side of a loved one far away instantly just by thinking about that person.

You may be able to communicate telepathically to let them know you are leaving and to say farewell until you meet again on the other side.

Take some time now to do these things while you have this opportunity between worlds.

PAUSE and give the person and yourself what ever time he and you need before continuing — it's ok to leave the room briefly.

As your life force leaves your physical body, your feet and hands may feel tingly as if they have gone to sleep.

As your life force leaves your physical body, it may feel fluid, like melting wax slowly spreading outward.

As your consciousness begins to expand beyond the physical world, you begin to remember.

You remember that you have done this before... that you are going home... that human life was a temporary condition ... that human life was one part of your whole life... that you are both human and divine ... that you and your soul are one with God.

You may hear buzzing noises, high pitched

whistling or low rolling thunder as your life force leaves your body.

You may experience heavenly visions or distorted images that rise and fade away.

When you focus on finding the Light, there is nothing to fear and all will fade away when the Clear Light appears

Imagine a bright, pulsating beam of light emanating from your lower body upwards with increasing momentum through the center of your body on a course to burst out through the top of your head.

Just before your heart stops beating, you will burst into full consciousness as the Clear Light dawns. Know that this is who you truly are and the Source of your being.

You will feel pulled toward it into a vortex of lights as if you are traveling through space at the speed of light, and you will go directly into the Light.

A Being of Light who knows all about you and loves you unconditionally may join you.

When you merge with the Light you will feel peace and love, and be filled with joy and happiness.

When you merge with the Light, you will meet with your loved ones on the other side.

Your loved ones will be there to welcome you home and there will be much celebrating over your graduation from earth university.

When you go into the Light, everything you didn't understand will become clear and you will be filled with peace and joy and reassurance that God is even more love than you ever imagined.

When you merge with the Light, you will know that you are Home.

NOTE: Before repeating Part 1, allow the person some quiet time to work through the process on her own, shift to telepathic communication in later stages and keep her on track by offering occasional positive words of encouragement, such as:

You are doing well.

You are focusing your attention on moving the light upwards.

You are letting go of any thoughts or desires about the material world.

You are free to go to your friends and loved ones and say your goodbyes.

Quickly use your relaxation exercise to lower your vibratory rate and attempt to communicate with your loved ones one last time.

You are able to raise your vibration, let go of the material world and move into the Light when you are ready.

You know whatever images arise are thought-forms from your own mind and will simply fade away.

Your journey is free of distractions and you are able to keep your focus on finding the Light.

Your soul drifts further away from your body and closer to the spiritual dimension.

You are feeling God's love all around you.

You are feeling lighter and lighter as you let go of your material desires... your physical attractions.

You are seeing now what is really important and realizing the lessons those desires and attractions had to teach you to help you on your spiritual journey.

You are seeing yourself as the beautiful spiritual being that you are and always were... you now see your self as a perfect child of God, filled with love and peace and joy.

Go now and merge with the Clear Light, your True Nature... become one with the Light... become one with Source / God / Totality / All That Is / Universal Intelligence.

Phrases similar to these or from scripture or other religious poems can also be used during the last few minutes of life and intermittently for the first few minutes after death.

About 5 minutes after death, begin reading some of Part 1 again for about 20 minutes; perhaps a modified version, urging the soul to stay on course, to ignore distractions, to visit loved ones and say their last goodbyes, and go immediately into the Clear Light when it dawns.

NOTES · NOTES · NOTES · NOTES · NOTES

Personal Transition Guidebook

(Sample)

PART 2

If you sense the person was unable to merge with the Light, begin reading Part 2 for about 20 minutes and occasionally thereafter for several days.

You have been through an amazing experience but the journey is not yet over.

Any initial bewilderment at what you are experiencing may quickly turn to astonishment because everything is so real, so natural, so perfect.

You may find it difficult to believe that you are dead because you feel very much alive.

You may wonder if you are dreaming, but you are not.

Just when you thought your life was over, you awakened to find you are still here... and you may have forgotten what to do next.

Listen to the sound of my voice.

Listen to these words ... these are your words as you have written them.

Your body is being taken care of as you directed ... your family knows your last wishes and abides by them ... your family will miss you and cry for you and have arguments concerning you but they will never forget you ... it is time for you to let go.

You may find yourself longing to return to your physical body, to your human life, to your loved ones, to your material possessions ... if it were not your time to return to the light, you would have been sent back ... this is your time.

You have said your goodbyes and made amends to the extent you were able ... you are free of excess emotional baggage ... you have learned what you came to learn and lightened your burden.

It is time for you to leave this dimension ... time to move on ... time to go into the light where there is no time, only God's unconditional love, waiting for you.

Recall your relaxation exercise to relax your whole being as your transformation from a physical to a spiritual being, your transition from the physical dimension to the spiritual dimension, progresses.

Focus on your light energy and notice if it is stuck somewhere ... if it is, focus on the area where it is blocked and move the energy by letting go of the physical attachment holding you back.

Move the light energy upward ... when you see the red light, direct the energy upward and let go of your attachments to physical gratification.

When you see the orange light, direct the energy upward and let go of your attachments to your fears, anger, hatred, greed, jealousy, angst.

When you see the yellow light, direct the energy upward and let go of your attachments to your emotions and anxieties.

When you see the green light, direct the energy upward and open your heart center to the love that surrounds you. Allow God's love to fill you up.

When you see the blue light, direct the energy upward and accept the truth about your self and the life you have just departed ... it was a perfect learning experience for your soul growth.

Allow this new understanding to expand your consciousness as you see the indigo light and direct the energy upwards ... everything you never understood will suddenly make complete sense to you ... you will remember everything you forgot when you became human.

Now that you see who you truly are and that you are both human and divine, you are prepared to merge with the Secondary Light when it dawns for you.

Continue to move the energy upwards toward the purple light at the top of your head as you let go of more and more of your attachments to the physical world ... open your consciousness to the wonders and the beauty of the spiritual world that lies just beyond the veil.

Let go.

Let go and let God.

Let go.

Reach out for the hand of the Being of Light who waits for you to merge with the Light. Focus on seeing your spiritual transition guide.

You are letting go of your insatiable wants and needs and desires about the physical world, and realize how little of it was really important now.

You are opening your heart to God's love.

God's love overwhelms you with ecstasy.

You recognize who you really are and accept yourself as God accepts you and loves you.

You realize you are a spiritual being and that you are leaving your human life behind to return to your spiritual home and family for the benefit of your spiritual growth.

You feel Unconditional Love all around you, within you, throughout All That Is.

Your spirit, your soul, and you are one with God.

You are in the Ultimate Light and the Ultimate Light is within you.

(PAUSE — 5 to 10 minutes)

If you haven't yet merged with the Secondary Light, you will have another opportunity following your life review.

You will find yourself viewing a movie about your life.

In the beginning, you will see all the loving, caring, kind things you did for others ... all the wonderful times you experienced with your loved ones ... all the meaningful things you accomplished in your life ... all the love and compassion you showed to others.

Next you will view any negative things you did during your lifetime ... all the cruelties you may have inflicted on others ... all the harsh words you may have spoken ... all your misplaced anger and aggression ... crimes you may have committed against others.

All your unkind and angry thoughts against others will all come back at you and force you to look at yourself and remember why you had to become human to learn to express compassion with your whole being.

Your soul will experience whatever pain you caused others during your human life to understand how it feels.

This is not a judgment to decide punishment, but an opportunity for your soul to view its human life from a higher perspective ... an opportunity to learn what you failed to see in yourself as a human being ... an opportunity to make changes and become a better human being next time around.

Your soul benefits from lessons you learned during this human lifetime and integrates the new information to evolve in consciousness and raise its vibration so you are able to exist in higher frequencies of the Light.

The lessons you are learning during your life review are contributing to your soul growth.

There is nothing to fear ... no-thing can harm you.

Continue to look for the Light and go to it when it appears before you.

Your soul development will continue on the other side with the support of your spiritual family who are waiting for you to merge with the Light and return Home.

Let go of your addictions and attractions to the physical world.

Detach from your wants and desires.

Let go of your emotions.

Detach from your intellect.

Let go of your physical body.

Everything you ever dreamed of, you will discover on the other side in a more rarefied form, more beautiful than you ever imagined.

Let go.

Trust.

Believe.

Have faith.

Be love.

Let go and merge with the Light.

Be at peace.

Go to the Light.

Become one with the Light.

Let go into the Light of Divine Love.

Epilogue

Reading this book and practicing dying consciously according to one's own spiritual or religious beliefs before dying, teaches us to live consciously — aware that we are at all times a breath away from making our transition, but able to live our lives fully, peacefully, without fear; prepared — mentally, emotionally and spiritually — for our transition whenever it comes.

Having the recommended conversations with loved ones, and practicing the easy meditation and guided visualization exercises will bring you to a new level of awareness about who you are and the meaning of your life on earth. This practice will assist you in reconciling your life, practicing forgiveness, healing your heart, and finding inner peace by connecting your human-self to your Soul-Self to consciously experience Unity, or Oneness, before you leave your body.

It involves the authoring of your Personal Transition Guidebook in your own words according to your own values and beliefs, to guide your soul through a peaceful transition into the Divine Light of Unconditional Love. It encourages families to have the conversations they need to have, and brings them closer together during these last precious moments and through their grieving process.

Whether you are the one who is dying or you are the caregiver, a family member or a friend of someone who may soon be involved in their transition process, these insights will give you the inner strength and compassion to help each other go through this very profound and loving experience, peacefully and mindfully.

Peace & Joy!

Diane

❧

Now the words are over
and the pain they bring are gone.
Now you have gone to rest
in the arms of the Beloved.

~ Rumi

NOTES · NOTES · NOTES · NOTES · NOTES

NOTES · NOTES · NOTES · NOTES · NOTES

Appendix

Life Review Topics

Death With Dignity Laws in the U.S.
* Oregon Death With Dignity Law
* Provisions of Washington Initiative
* Vermont Law on Immunity for Terminally Ill
* Montana Opinion: the "Rights of the Terminally Ill"

Egyptian Book of the Dead

The Bardo Thodol — from The Tibetan Book of the Dead

The Blind Men and the Elephant

Life Review Topics

These are some of the topics a transition guide might suggest as part of an oral, written or videotaped history to be left for the family. They often lead to deeper discussions involving the whole family. These may help you or your patients work toward acceptance of the end of this life and more openness to learning the practice of conscious dying into the continuation of life.

- Your family of origin
- Childhood dreams
- Friends and lovers
- Marriage and family; children, grandchildren, great-grandchildren
- Extended family
- Genealogy
- Historical events in your lifetime, important people
- Countries, states, towns lived in/visited
- Schools attended, honors, awards, sports
- Hobbies, sports, other activities through life
- Travel (domestic, foreign), local adventures
- Religious background
- The role of money in your life
- Your education
- Your career or life work, accomplishments, awards
- Jobs, positions you held, sole proprietorships
- Military service
- Community service, Volunteer work
- Retirement
- Major life lessons/challenges
- Your beliefs, values, philosophy. political views
- Your health and body, major illnesses, surgeries, accidents

- Your sexual identity/attitudes/problems
- Drug/alcohol use/abuse
- Police record, criminal activities
- Traumatic experiences, fears
- Vehicles in your life
- Favorite books? movies? TV shows? games?
- Pets in your life
- Your experiences and ideas about death
- Your spiritual life and values
- Your goals and aspirations
- What is your greatest accomplishment?
- Who or what are you most grateful for?
- What are your most embarrassing moments?
- What were your biggest disappointments in life?
- What brought you the greatest joy?
- What do you regret?
- What are you ashamed of?
- What are you most proud of?
- Who were your role models or heroes?
- Who made you laugh the hardest?
- Best/worst time in your life
- What did you learn?
- Who did you love unconditionally?
- Who loved you unconditionally?
- Were you kind?
- Did you help others?
- Do you have any regrets?
- Would you change anything about your life?
- Words of wisdom to pass down?

ം

Death With Dignity Laws in the U.S.

Oregon Death With Dignity Law

Under the law, a capable adult Oregon resident who has been diagnosed, by a physician, with a terminal illness that will kill the patient within six months may request in writing, from his physician, a prescription for a lethal dose of medication for the purpose of ending the patient's life. Exercise of the option under this law is voluntary and the patient must initiate the request. Any physician, pharmacist or healthcare provider who has moral objections may refuse to participate.

The request must be confirmed by two witnesses, at least one of whom is not related to the patient, is not entitled to any portion of the patient's estate, is not the patient's physician, and is not employed by a health care facility caring for the patient. After the request is made, another physician must examine the patient's medical records and confirm the diagnosis. The patient must be determined to be free of a mental condition impairing judgment. If the request is authorized, the patient must wait at least fifteen days and make a second oral request before the prescription may be written. The patient has a right to rescind the request at any time. Should either physician have concerns about the patient's ability to make an informed decision, or feel the patient's request may be motivated by depression or coercion, the patient must be referred for a psychological evaluation.

The law protects doctors from liability for providing a lethal prescription for a terminally ill, competent adult in compliance with the statute's restrictions. Participation by physicians, pharmacists, and health care providers is voluntary. The law also specifies a patient's decision to end his or her life shall not "have an effect upon a life, health, or accident insurance or annuity policy."

Provisions of Washington Initiative
The official ballot summary for the measure, slightly amended following a February 2008 court challenge, is, "This measure would permit terminally ill, competent, adult Washington residents medically predicted to die within six months to request and self-administer lethal medication prescribed by a physician. The measure requires two oral and one written request, two physicians to diagnose the patient and determine the patient is competent, a waiting period, and physician verification of an informed patient decision. Physicians, patients and others acting in good faith compliance would have criminal and civil immunity."

Provisions in the law include:
- The patient must be an adult (18 or over) resident of the state of Washington.
- The patient must be mentally competent, verified by two physicians (or referred to a mental health evaluation).
- The patient must be terminally ill with less than 6 months to live, verified by two physicians.
- The patient must make voluntary requests, without coercion, verified by two physicians.
- The patient must be informed of all other options including palliative and hospice care.
- There is a 15-day waiting period between the first oral request and a written request.
- There is a 48-hour waiting period between the written request and the writing of the prescription.

- Two independent witnesses must sign the written request, at least one of who is not related to the patient or employed by the health care facility.
- The patient is encouraged to discuss with family (not required because of confidentiality laws).
- The patient may change their mind at any time and rescind the request.
- The attending physician may sign the patient's death certificate, which must list the underlying terminal disease as the cause of death.

Vermont Law on Immunity for Terminally Ill

(1) "Bona fide health care professional-patient relationship" means a treating or consulting relationship in the course of which a health care professional has completed a full assessment of the patient's medical history and current medical condition, including a personal physical examination.

(2) "Health care professional" means an individual licensed to practice medicine under 26 V.S.A. chapter 23 or 33.

(3) "Terminal condition" means an incurable and irreversible disease which would, within reasonable medical judgment, result in death within six months.

(b) A health care professional who has a bona fide health care professional-patient relationship with a patient with a terminal condition and who prescribes medication to that patient for the relief of symptoms associated with or caused by the terminal condition shall not be subject to criminal or civil liability or professional disciplinary action if the patient self-administers more than a prescribed dosage of the medication and dies as a result.

(c) A person shall not be subject to criminal or civil liability solely for being present when a patient self-administers a lethal dose of a medication that has been prescribed for that patient by a health care professional.

Montana Opinion on the "Rights of the Terminally Ill"
The opinion of the court reads, in part:

... we find no indication in Montana law that physician aid in dying provided to terminally ill, mentally competent adult patients is against public policy.

... a physician who aids a terminally ill patient in dying is not directly involved in the final decision or the final act. He or she only provides a means by which a terminally ill patient himself can give effect to his life-ending decision, or not, as the case may be. Each stage of the physician-patient interaction is private, civil, and compassionate. The physician and terminally ill patient work together to create a means by which the patient can be in control of his own mortality. The patient's subsequent private decision whether to take the medicine does not breach public peace or endanger others.

The Rights of the Terminally Ill Act very clearly provides that terminally ill patients are entitled to autonomous, end of life decisions, even if enforcement of those decisions involves direct acts by a physician. Furthermore, there is no indication in the Rights of the Terminally Ill Act that an additional means of giving effect to a patient's decision —in which the patient, without any direct assistance, chooses the time of his own death — is against public policy.

In conclusion, we find nothing in Montana Supreme Court precedent or Montana statutes indicating that physician aid in dying is against public policy.

Egyptian Book of the Dead

A 17-foot long papyrus scroll was found buried with a 70-year old woman named Nany, who was a ritual singer of the god Amun-Ra. It contained hieroglyphics depicting her expected journey into the After Life.

At the climax of her journey, Nany is in the Hall of Judgment. She is holding her mouth and her eyes in her hands as she stands to the left of a large arm-balance scale. Her heart is being weighed against Maat, the goddess of justice and truth, who is represented as a tiny figure wearing her symbol, a single large feather in her headband.

On the right, Osiris, god of the underworld and rebirth, presides over the scene. He wears the white crown of Upper Egypt and the curving beard of a god. His body is wrapped like a mummy except for his hands, which clasp a crook. On the table before him is an offering of a joint of beef.

Jackal-headed Anubis, overseer of mummification, adjusts the scales, while a baboon — symbolizing Thoth, the god of wisdom and writing — sits on the balance beam and prepares to write down the result. Behind Nany stands the goddess Isis, both wife and sister of Osiris.

In the next scene, Nany has been found truthful and therefore worthy of entering the afterlife. Anubis says to Osiris, "Her heart is an accurate witness," and Osiris replies, "Give her her eyes and mouth, since her heart is an accurate witness."

A creature with a crocodile head, which was called

the Devourer of Souls, swallowed heavy hearts. The good people were led to the Happy Fields, where they joined Osiris. Many spells and rituals were designed to ensure a favorable judgment and were written in the papyrus or linen "Book of the Dead." These scenes were later depicted on the walls of the tombs of kings and people of high rank.

Most important for full participation in the afterlife was the need for an individual's identity to be preserved. They believed the body housed the ka, or soul, and had to be preserved for the soul to live on. Consequently, the body had to remain intact and receive regular offerings of food and drink.

The Bardo Thodol

Liberation through Hearing in the Intermediate State
from
The Tibetan Book of the Dead

Thou wilt pay undistracted attention to that with which I am about to set thee face to face, and hold on;

O nobly-born, that which is called death hath now come. Thou art departing from this world, but thou are not the only one; [death] cometh to all. Do not cling, in fondness and weakness, to this life. Even though thou clingest out of weakness, thou hast not the power to remain here. Thou wilt gain nothing more than wandering in this Samsara. Be not attached [to this world]; be not weak.

O nobly-born, when thy body and mind were separating, thou must have experienced a glimpse of the Pure Truth, subtle, sparkling, bright dazzling, glorious, and radiantly awesome, in appearance like a mirage moving across a landscape in spring-time in one continuous stream of vibrations. Be not daunted thereby, nor terrified, nor awed. That is the radiance of thine own true nature. Recognize it.

From the midst of that radiance, the natural sound of Reality, reverberating like a thousand thunders simultaneously sounding, will come. That is the natural sound of thine own real self. Be not daunted thereby, nor terrified, nor awed.

The body, which thou hast now is called the thought-body of propensities. Since thou hast not a material body of flesh and blood, whatever may come — sounds, lights,

or rays — are all three unable to harm thee; thou art
incapable of dying. It is quite sufficient for thee to know
that these apparitions are thine own thought-forms.
Recognize this to be the Bardo.

NOTES · NOTES · NOTES · NOTES · NOTES

The Blind Men and the Elephant

It was six men of Indostan
To learning much inclined
Who went to see the elephant
(Though all of them were blind),
That each by observation
Might satisfy his mind.

The First approached the elephant,
And happening to fall
Against his broad and sturdy side,
At once began to bawl:
"God Bless me! but the elephant
Is nothing but a wall!"

The Second feeling of the tusk,
Cried: "Ho! What have we here
So very round and smooth and sharp?
To me 'tis mighty clear
This wonder of an elephant
Is very like a spear!"

The Third approached the animal,
And happening to take
The squirming trunk within his hands,
Thus boldly up and spake:
"I see," quoth he, "The elephant
Is very like a snake!"

The Fourth reached out his eager hand
And felt about the knee:
"What most this wondrous beast is like

Is mighty plain," quoth he;
" 'Tis clear enough the elephant
Is very like a tree."

The Fifth, who chanced to touch the ear,
Said: "Even the blindest man
Can tell what this resembles most;
Deny the fact who can,
This marvel of an elephant
Is very like a fan!"

The Sixth no sooner had begun
About the beast to grope,
Than, seizing on the swinging tail
That fell within his scope,
"I see," quoth he, "The elephant
Is very like a rope!"

And so these men of Indostan
Disputed loud and long,
Each in his own opinion
Exceeding stiff and strong,
Though each was partly in the right
And all were in the wrong!

So oft in theologic wars
The disputants, I ween,
Rail on in utter ignorance
Of what each other mean,
And prat about an elephant
Not one of them has seen!
    ~ John Godfrey Saxe (1816-1877)

NOTES · NOTES · NOTES · NOTES · NOTES

Bibliography

Atwater, P.M.H. *We Live Forever: The Truth About Death.* A.R.E. Press, 2004.

Callanan, Maggie and Patricia Kelley. *Final Gifts: Understanding the Special Awareness, Needs and Communications of the Dying.* Bantam Books, 1993.

Chopra, Deepak. *Life After Death.* Three Rivers Press, 2003.

Collins, Kelsey. *Exit Strategy: Leaving this Life with Grace and Gratitude.* ChaseHawk Publishing, 2008.

Daniel, Terri. *Embracing Death.* O Books, 2010.

Fenwick, Peter and Elizabeth Fenwick. *The Art of Dying.* Continuum, 2008.

Greyson, Bruce, PhD. *The Handbook of Near-Death Experiences: Thirty Years of Investigation.* Praeger, 2009.

Kervorkian, Jack, M.D. *Prescription: Medicide: The Goodness of a Planned Death.* Prometheus Books, 1993.

Kubler-Ross, M.D., Elisabeth. *On Death and Dying: What the Dying Have to Teach Doctors, Nurses, Clergy and their Own Families.* Tavistock Publications, 1976.

Long, Jeffrey. *Evidence of the Afterlife: The Science of Near-Death Experiences.* Harper One, 2010.

Moody, Raymond, M.D. *Glimpses of Eternity: Sharing a Loved Ones Passage From This Life to the Next.* Guideposts, 2010.

Moody, M.D., Raymond. *Life After Life.* Guideposts, 1975

Morse, Melvin, M.D. *Closer to the Light: Learning from the Near-Death Experiences of Children.* Ivy Books, 1990.

Parnia, M.D., Sam. *What Happens When We Die: A Groundbreaking Study into the Nature of Life and Death.* Hay House, 2010.

Ring, Kenneth, PHD. *Lessons From the Light.* Moment Point Press, 2006.

Van Lommel, Pim, M.D. *Consciousness Beyond Life: The Science of the Near-Death Experience.* Harper One, 2011.

Varga, Josie. *Visits to Heaven.* 4th Dimension Press, 2010.

Recommended Musical Soundscapes

Healing, ShapeshifterDNA/Gary & JoAnn Chambers, Visionary Music.com 1986

Odyssey Chakra Balancing, ShapeshifterDNA/Gary & JoAnn Chambers, VisionaryMusic.com 1989

Journey of the Soul, ShapeshifterDNA/Gary & JoAnn Chambers, VisionaryMusic.com 2009

Journey towards Ascension, ShapeshifterDNA/Gary & JoAnn Chambers, VisionaryMusic.com 2007

ৡৢ

Other Works by Diane Goble

**Search author name/title
at most online ebook retailers**

Reincarnation and the Evolution of Consciousness (ebook), 2013

The Path to Peace & Joy: a practical meditation, 2013 (ebook)

How to Die Consciously: Secrets from Beyond the Veil, 2011 (1st Edition, ebook)

Conversations with a Near-Death Experiencer: Book 1, 2010 (ebook)

More Conversations with a Near-Death Experiencer: Book 2, 2010 (ebook)

Sitting in the Lotus Blossom, 2010 (ebook)

·

Relaxation Meditation and Guided Imagery downloads
available at www.BeyondtheVeil.net

·

Beginner's Guide to Conscious Dying, 2009 (out-of-print)

Through the Tunnel: A Traveller's Guide to Spiritual Rebirth, 1993 (out-of-print)

৩৵৶

About Diane Goble

Diane returned to college 7 years after her near-death/afterlife experience and earned a Master's degree in Community Psychology (CSULB) and 7 years later another in Clinical Hypnotherapy (St. John's U, LA). She was a pioneer in the field of stress management in the 1980s as an educator and human resources consultant. She practiced as a hypnotherapist and past-life regression therapist, and as a spiritual counselor. She was a hospice volunteer off and on for over 20 years in Florida, California and Oregon. She often supplemented her income as a graphic artist, a landscape photographer and a writer. She developed a Transition Guide Training program to certify professionals to teach the Art of Conscious Dying. She created her first website, A Near-Death Experience Beyond the Veil in 1996, which she continues to maintain. She is the author of eight nonfiction books in the field of death and dying. She has lived in New York, Florida, Nassau, Illinois, Colorado, California and currently lives in Sisters, Oregon where she writes articles for her local newspaper and a blog, "Let's talk about death and dying..." She is also an advocate for Compassion & Choices and Death with Dignity laws.

Diane would love to hear from readers, and offers email and personal consultations. Please send email to her at cosmiccreativity@mac.com and visit BeyondtheVeil.net.

NOTES · NOTES · NOTES · NOTES · NOTES

NOTES · NOTES · NOTES · NOTES · NOTES

NOTES · NOTES · NOTES · NOTES · NOTES

NOTES · NOTES · NOTES · NOTES · NOTES

NOTES · NOTES · NOTES · NOTES · NOTES

NOTES · NOTES · NOTES · NOTES · NOTES

CPSIA information can be obtained
at www.ICGtesting.com
Printed in the USA
LVHW091911191121
703841LV00006B/25

9 780963 860651